An Accidental Anarchist

how the killing of a humble Jewish immigrant by Chicago's chief of police exposed the conflict between law & order and civil rights in early 20th-century America

WALTER ROTH AND JOE KRAUS

Rudi Publishing
San Francisco

Rudi Publishing
12 Geary St. #508
San Francisco, CA 94108
(415)392-6940

ISBN 0-945213-23-9 (paper)
ISBN 0-945213-24-7 (hardcover)

Printed in the United States of America
Vaughan Printing, Nashville, Tennessee

Library of Congress Cataloging-in-Publication Data

Roth, Walter,
    An accidental anarchist : how the killing of a humble Jewish immi-
grant by Chicago's chief of police exposed the conflict between law &
order and civil rights in early 20th-century America / Walter Roth and
Joe Kraus.
        p. cm.
    Includes bibliographical references and index.
    ISBN 0-945213-24-7 (hardcover). — ISBN 0-945213-23-9 (paper)
    1. Murder—Illinois—Chicago. 2. Immigrants—Illinois—Chicago.
3. Averbuch, Lazarus, d. 1908. 4. Chicago (Ill.)—History—1875-
5. Chicago (Ill.)—Social conditions. I. Kraus, Joe .
II. Title.
HV6534.C4R67 1997
977.3'11041—dc21   97-52551
                                              CIP

Cover design by Kristin Boekhoff

CONTENTS

ACKNOWLEDGMENTS

We owe thanks to many people in helping us put this book together. We thank our families—Walter's wife Chaya and their children Ari and Kate; Judy and Steven; and Mark and Miriam (who spent a summer helping with the research for this book); Richard, June, Edward, and Amy Kraus; and Paula Chaiken—for their understanding and patience as we fought with each other every step of the way. We thank Charles Bernstein, Irwin Suloway, and Norman Schwartz of the Chicago Jewish Historical Society for their help and encouragement; Joseph "Andy" Hays for his assistance; and Alex Bogdanovitch, Bill Huston, and Ray Marx for their support. We also thank Terri Boekhoff and the people of Rudi Publishing—Michael Huston, Kristin Boekhoff, Brien Woods, and David Featherstone—for their belief in this project and their many efforts to strengthen our manuscript. Finally, we acknowledge the invaluable assistance of Dr. Zanville Klein for his Yiddish translations, and we hope that this book can serve as a testament to his memory.

PREFACE

The story of the Averbuch Affair—the story of the little we know about a young man named either Lazarus or Jeremiah Averbuch[1]—has a hole in its middle. We know a great deal about what took place around the killing of the young Russian Jewish immigrant in 1908, but we know almost nothing about the event itself. This is a murder mystery, but who intended to kill whom and for what motive remain unanswerable questions. We know that Averbuch wound up dead and we know that George Shippy admitted firing the fatal bullets, but that is almost all we know about the central moment of the affair. We don't know what brought Averbuch to a place as far from his own world as Shippy's home. We don't know what Shippy thought as he saw a foreign-looking man on his doorstep. And, in the end, we don't know who Averbuch really was.

We set out to recount the story of Averbuch's killing with two competing impulses in mind. First, we approached it as a mystery that has never received due attention. We tried to present all of the evidence in the case; some of it, particularly information from Harold Ickes's papers, has only recently been made public. Although the Averbuch Affair frequently occurs as a footnote in larger histories, the only previous work devoted to it completely is a 1972 article by James Rudin.[2] Many of the individuals caught up in the affair—including Jane Addams, Emma Goldman, Ben Reitman, Harold Ickes, Oscar Straus, Bernard Horwich, and Philip Bregstone—wrote about it in their memoirs or left observations of it that their biographers picked up, but we are not aware of any work that pulls together as wide a range of material on the affair as we attempt to do.

Our second impulse was to trace the way the story of Averbuch was contested in the American public of 1908. To the Chicago represented by Fred Busse and George Shippy, immigrants were often foreign, different, and frightening. To the immigrant community that housed Olga Averbuch, the America outside its boundaries often seemed alien and threatening; in the case of Averbuch himself, it proved fatal. At the heart of the Averbuch Affair is a collision of those two very different communities. As newspaper reporters, social critics, political activists, government officials, and Americanized Jews told and retold the story of what happened when Averbuch went to Shippy's home, they spoke at the same time of their hopes for what Chicago—indeed what all of America—could be. Even if we leave the murder mystery largely unsolved, we hope to have shown what was at stake for the different people of Chicago as the city tried to make sense of a senseless affair.

In researching the case, we relied as much as possible on newspaper reports and the handful of other reports about the affair, drawing heavily from such mainstream newspapers as the *Chicago Daily News, Chicago Evening American, Chicago Daily Journal, Chicago Record-Herald, Chicago Tribune, Inter Ocean*

(Chicago) and *New York Times*; from such parochial newspapers as the *Chicago Daily Socialist* and Yiddish newspapers such as the *Daily Forward*, *Daily Courier* (Chicago), and *Morning Journal* (New York); and from such contemporary magazines as *The Public*, *The Reform Advocate*, and *Mother Earth*. We attempted to situate the discussion about the affair within its historical moment by using other historical works, but our emphasis throughout was to record the story as its actors attempted to tell it. At times we quoted liberally from our sources in an effort to let the voices of 1908 reenact their fight to control the story of Averbuch and Shippy. We hope such lengthy quotations do not distract from either our analysis or the drama that played itself out as the period before the final inquest drew to a close. We hope, rather, that those voices, with all of their passions and fears, will help bring alive the fact that more than justice for Averbuch was at stake; the hole in the middle of the Averbuch Affair was the question of not merely what happened to the young man, but also of who could be an American in the Chicago of 1908.

—Walter Roth and Joe Kraus

July, 1997

I

TWO CITIES CALLED CHICAGO

March 2, 1908

Chicago started the twentieth century as two different cities. There was the Chicago that had flowered in the wake of the great fire in 1871. Its citizens were the prosperous merchants, bankers, industrialists, and politicians who had shaped the business district and fashionable lakeshore neighborhoods and who held unchallenged political power. They established most of Chicago's newspapers, bankrolled construction of the city's great buildings and industries, and laid out the basic blueprint that has directed Chicago's growth ever since. Most of them were born in the United States, and many had moved to Chicago from other parts of the country. They tried to make Chicago and its government in their image—a blend of East Coast dignity and Puritanism with a frontier consciousness—and, for a time perhaps, they succeeded.

The other Chicago was the city Carl Sandburg would celebrate. Its citizens were the many impoverished laborers and newly arrived immigrants who toiled in railroad depots, shipyards, and factories. Those thousands, added to by the relentless stream of immigrants, made up the bulk of the city's population. When fortunate, they lived in the less densely populated areas of the city. When less fortunate, they squeezed themselves into the ghettos and row houses of downtown and the west side of the Chicago River. Although their individual names are remembered less frequently than the gentry's, they too took part in shaping Chicago. They are the ones who eventually developed the many neighborhoods for which the city is known. They are the ones whose labor built the canals, roads, and buildings. And they are the ones who, through their unions and organizations, gave part of their image to the city: the tough, blue collar, big shouldered identity by which Chicago is still known.

By 1908, the city abounded in contrasts that reflected the coming together of the two Chicagos. Along the lakeshore it had its many new buildings, new auditorium, museums, palatial homes, and elevated train system. Just inland were the slums, full of the gambling, drinking, and prostitution for which the city was equally well known. Its downtown Loop area was one of the world's great markets, but less than a mile west across the river was such poverty that Jane Addams located her Hull House settlement there. As close as the two Chicagos were geographically, they were inhabited by widely disparate societies. On March 2, 1908, the two Chicagos collided in an unprecedented way. That morning, the city brought together—for one fatal, mysterious moment—Lazarus Averbuch and George Shippy.

Chicago didn't give a young man like Lazarus Averbuch many choices, not that he could have anticipated many. He was nineteen years old and had never been free of oppression. He grew up in Kishinev, Russia, where he was a Jewish subject of the capricious government of Czar Nicholas II. In 1905, he and his family survived the Kishinev pogrom, a vicious attack on the Jewish community of that city in which hundreds were killed or wounded.

The Averbuch family fled to Czernowitz, Bukovina, part of the Austro-Hungarian empire, but looked ultimately to the United States as the place to build their lives. In Austria, Lazarus worked as a bookkeeper and studied when he had time. When he reached Chicago in late 1907, he was fluent in several languages and at least partially literate in English. As

Fig. 1. Lazarus Averbuch residence.
Photograph: *Chicago Daily News.* Chicago Historical Society. DN–005869.

one of many Jewish immigrants pouring into the country at the
time, though, he would find little use for what education he had
been able to give himself.

He settled on the west side of Chicago, in the Jewish ghetto,
with his sister Olga. Her small apartment at 218 Washburne Avenue was home not just to the two siblings, but also to Rose Stern,
Olga's friend and a subtenant. They probably paid between $6
and $10 a month in rent, a sizable amount considering Olga
earned only about $40 a month and her brother little more than
$30. Olga, two years older than her brother, had been in the city
for nearly eighteen months and had begun to know her way. She
had lived for some time at the Miriam Club, a school for young
Jewish immigrant girls, where she was taught some English and
given help settling in the new country.[3] By the time Lazarus arrived, Olga was working as a self-described "sewing woman" in
what we would today call a sweatshop. She claimed to be saving
almost $15 a month and had achieved a kind of stability in her
new life in Chicago.

Their apartment building, a two-story frame house, was typical of the area around Twelfth and Halsted streets at that time.
They were close to the Maxwell Street market, where Jews and
other immigrant groups sold everything from fresh foods to trin-
kets to rags and bottles. During the final two decades of the nineteenth century, over 50,000 Jews moved into the area, and the
number was increasing as the twentieth century began. The neighborhood was the sort of place where only children could be
counted on to know English. Yiddish was spoken everywhere, as
were the many other languages of the varying eastern and southern European countries from which the immigrants had come. It
was possible here, and indeed common, to wear "old country" clothing. There were synagogues and kosher food stores all around, so it
was possible to live without ever needing to leave the area.

Lazarus Averbuch had hoped to find work as a bookkeeper in the city. He had done such work in Austria and had a reputation as being at least a solid student. He worked instead for a brief time in Tony Rubovitz's book bindery on Plymouth Place before going to work for W. H. Eichengreen as an egg packer at 183 South Water Street. Neither position satisfied him, however. He worked long hours at hard, physical work and then, in the evenings, attended the Jewish Training School at 12th and Jefferson.[4] He earned less than his sister, which seemed to have troubled him.

Averbuch was hardly alone in his difficulty with finding satisfying work. Chicago was still feeling the effects of the depression of 1907. Such periodic economic breakdowns were common in America in the latter part of the nineteenth century and the beginning of the twentieth, but the 1907 depression was the most severe between the depressions of the middle 1880s and early 1890s and the Great Depression of the early 1930s. Chicago, which had seen tremendous growth in the years immediately preceding this recent downturn, was especially hard hit. Its many new and itinerant workers found likely sources of jobs drying up even as immigrants continued pouring into the city. Unprecedented numbers of unemployed people swelled the city and created what seemed to be a near-crisis situation.

Averbuch's dreams were undoubtedly the dreams of most immigrants. According to his sister, the two of them were saving what they could in order to pay for passage to Chicago for their parents and some of their siblings still in Czernowitz. According to some of his friends, Lazarus thought about leaving Chicago in search of a place with greater opportunities for him. At the Jewish Training School, he may well have heard about Abraham Levy's plan to help young Jewish immigrants get started as farmers in central Iowa.[5] He might also have heard the common rumors that there were opportunities to be had farther west, as far as California. How far he went with any of his plans is impossible to determine, but it is clear he was a man readying himself for something on the morning he set out to see George Shippy.

Chief of Police George Shippy was one of Chicago's most prominent figures. His world had originally been civic service, but he had risen to such an important post that he stood, by 1908, on equal footing with commercial and political leaders. Newspapers mentioned him regularly, and he basked in his reputation as a hardline law-and-order administrator. In his home at 21 North Lincoln Place—an old, prestigious northside area—he employed a live-in maid and a chauffeur. He was captain not simply to the police department but also, it seemed, to his family. Both his daughter Georgetta and his niece Georgina were named in his honor, and his son Harry, a student at Culver Academy, showed every indication of following in his footsteps.

Although Shippy had certainly never known the poverty Averbuch had, he had not always been so secure. His father was of Irish descent, had come to Chicago from New York in the early 1840s, and had embarked on a twenty-year career with the police department, eventually reaching the rank of lieutenant. Shippy himself began his career with the Chicago fire department. He was a large, strong man who, early in his career, won notoriety for his efficiency and toughness. In one incident he survived an accident that threw him off his hook and ladder truck and killed his partner. He left the fire department before long and, following three years in private life, joined the police force. Although he resigned from the force a few years later and went into business for himself, he rejoined it again in the middle 1890s. In 1907, Fred Busse, the newly elected mayor, selected Shippy for the top position.

From early in his career, Shippy seems to have been earmarked as someone who could handle the difficult political assignments. One of his first responsibilities was to stand security for former State's Attorney J. S. Grinnell, who was receiving death threats from anarchists outraged at his zealous prosecution of the men eventually executed for incendiary remarks that allegedly caused the bombing at Haymarket Square. Shippy served briefly as police captain at the opening of the World's Fair in 1893 and then directed a special mayoral escort squad on the occasion of a Spanish princess's visit later that year. The latter assignment was made more difficult by the concern that anarchists worldwide were committed to killing leaders of every sort. Those concerns were heightened by the subsequent assassinations of President McKinley in 1901, King Carlos of Portugal early in 1908, and numerous high-ranking officials of Czarist Russia throughout the early 1900s. In 1900, Shippy was assigned to assist in suppressing labor disturbances in Chicago.[6]

Whatever his political feelings were before his experiences on the police force, Shippy was a hardened foe of labor and social unrest by the time he became "the Chief." He had no patience for demonstrations growing out of the lot of the poor. There wasn't room in his Chicago for radical agitation. As he put it at one point, "Social settlements are first cousins to the anarchists." So saying, he implicated not just Jane Addams, but even such a mainstream political figure as Judge Julian Mack.[7]

By 1908, Chicago was the capital of American radicalism. As the site of the Haymarket Square protest in 1886, it was confirmed as the headquarters of anarchism in the United States.[8] The monument erected at Forest Park Cemetery, where the executed Haymarket anarchists were interred, served as a rallying shrine to the movement. Moreover, the bitter labor dispute against the Pullman Company in 1894 had established Chicago as a focal point in labor's efforts to organize workers in large cities. By the time Shippy became police chief in 1907, Chicago had one of the largest unemployed populations of any city in the country.[9] With the huge influx of European immigrants, many bringing the radical teachings of such thinkers as Michael Bakunin and Peter Kropotkin, Chicago proved to be a breeding ground for much of the activity Shippy abhorred.

Some kind of conflict between Shippy and groups supporting such causes was inevitable. On January 23, 1908, Ben Reitman, a physician and sometime self-professed hobo, led a "march of the unemployed" down LaSalle Street to the Board of Trade Building, the center of grain trading in the country. Subsequent police reports attempted to place Lazarus Averbuch at the march, but whether he was actually there is impossible to determine. The demonstration attracted several hundred participants, despite Shippy's threats that he would stop such a demonstration by force if necessary. By the day's end, Shippy had followed through with his threat. The march was dispersed and Reitman was clubbed and arrested. Shippy told the newspapers he was sorry the event had given so much attention to the labor movement, "but I did not intend to allow any anarchist gathering. I took the precautions I did merely to be sure of preventing anything worse occurring." There would not be, he made clear, any second Haymarket incident while he was in charge.[10]

Shippy's concerns as chief of police were not limited to radicals, however. Soon after his appointment, Chicago experienced its first criminal gang war. Although the conflict paled in comparison to the bloodshed that took place twenty years later when Prohibition and bootlegging held sway in Chicago, the war between rival gamblers Mont Tennes and James O'Leary set new standards for criminal violence at the time. At the turn of the century, Chicago gambling was controlled, essentially, by three rings: Tennes's to the north, and O'Leary's to the south; and, in the Loop, gamblers paid protection to First Ward committee member Mike "Hinky-Dink" Kenna and his cohorts. Through a series of Byzantine alliances and deceptions, Tennes came to be the dominant gambling chief as well as controller of the wire service that provided racetrack results to gambling joints across the city. O'Leary retaliated by bombing the home of a Tennes lieutenant. Before long, the gangs were exchanging bombs at a rate that terrorized the city.[11]

Shippy had begun his tenure with a wave of crackdowns on gambling sites and a widely cited declaration that he would stop gambling or "run all of the gamblers out of the city."[12] His men went so far as to close down, temporarily, one of Tennes's chief houses and arrest two of his henchmen. Those men, however, never went to trial, and the gambling houses recovered immediately and continued in full swing. By the time of the bombings in the early months of 1908, Shippy had grown curiously inactive. Maintaining, despite the evidence of the bombing war, that he had defeated gambling in the city, he said, "It looks as if there was a big gamblers' war on in Chicago. I still maintain, however, that there is no gambling worthy of the name in existence here at the present time."[13]

Explanation for that inaction probably went, according to reports collected by State's Attorney John J. Healy, beyond Shippy and on to Mayor Busse. Even before the turn of the century, Chicago had developed notoriety for its political corruption. The criminals and organizations that controlled gambling and prostitution soon came to control city government: it seemed to be a Chicago tradition. Kenna had been rumored to hand-pick mayors for over twenty years, and there was little reason to think criminal influence in government had diminished. By the beginning of 1908, Healy had put together an array of evidence that Shippy and Busse were somehow involved in protecting Tennes's ring.

On the morning of March 2, 1908, Shippy was a man with many concerns. Between his dealings with left-wing agitators, his underworld connections, and the impending investigation, he must have worried whether he could survive the political storm gathering around him. If he were to become a liability to Mayor Busse, he would lose his job. If he crossed some of these forces, he could lose even more. He would say later that he feared someone might be bold enough to come after him; bold enough, perhaps, to attack him in his own home.

When Lazarus Averbuch left his west side ghetto home that morning, he traveled into the other Chicago, a place where he was alien. His dark hair and clothing immediately labeled him as a foreigner. If he had occasion to speak, his accent would have betrayed him as well. He would have had difficulty reading the *Chicago Tribune*, a paper already making much of the differences between "immigrant races." An article in the paper a day earlier offered a chart describing the various noses of Chicago. "Chicago's typical nose," it declared, is "inclined to be Roman, especially in the average, young businessman; [it] has traces of the classic Greek and Hebrew, but Roman predominates, indicat[ing] hustle and combativeness." Of the handful of major Chicago figures whose noses the accompanying article singled out, it declared of Chief Shippy's nose that it was "Roman, pronounced, combative." Of a "Hebrew or Aquiline" nose (like Averbuch's) it wrote, "Generally a commercial nose; indicates suspicion, power of adaptation to surroundings and ability to look out for No. 1 in financial matters."

Averbuch's trip from Washburne Avenue to Lincoln Place could not have been an easy one, though some people stated that he made the same trip a day earlier, on Sunday, but had returned because no one was home at Shippy's house. He had to transfer from one streetcar to another on a bitterly cold, wintery day. He had to pass through areas that must have been unfamiliar to him. He probably had to pay a five cent fare, a not inconsiderable sum for someone trying to save every penny. And it probably took

Fig. 2. Chief Shippy's residence.
Photograph: *Chicago Daily News.* Chicago Historical Society. DN–005941.

him a full hour and a half to complete the trip. Eventually, however, he stood before Chief Shippy's door and rang.

Within ten minutes of his knocking, Averbuch was dead. He had been shot six times. Shippy was wounded, how seriously is unclear. Shippy's son Harry would need to be hospitalized from gunshot wounds, and his driver, James Foley, was wounded. The newspapers had a story. Chicago had a mystery.

II

READ ALL ABOUT IT

THE OFFICIAL STORY EMERGES

March 3–4

The city was stunned by Averbuch's killing. Within hours on that cold Monday morning it was front page news, and for days it remained a source of citywide anxiety. Various reports described different and startling aspects of the killing and about Averbuch. It took at least thirty-six hours before the city's several mainstream newspapers reached any consensus on what had taken place, and many of the discarded stories confused and alarmed factions in the city. Even as an official story emerged, the city bordered on hysteria.

Chief Shippy stepped forward almost immediately with a prepared statement explaining what had taken place. His version underwent some changes in the days that followed, but it laid the foundations for what came to be the almost universally accepted version of what happened that morning. In a report he prepared before press time for that Monday's afternoon newspapers, Shippy wrote:

I had a premonition of this, and the attack on me came as no surprise. Therefore I have been on guard. My premonition that I was the object of an assassination plot was verified this morning. The first I knew was the ring on the doorbell about 9 o'clock. It might have been a few minutes earlier or it might have been a minute or two later. I answered in person and saw standing there a man who was evidently a Sicilian or an Armenian. He was about 26 years old. He said, "Is Chief Shippy in? I have an important letter for him."

With that he took out of his pocket an envelope addressed to George M. Shippy, Superintendent of Police, City Hall, Chicago or residence, 31 Lincoln Place.

I looked at the man and instead of taking the letter I grasped his arm. With that he struggled.

My wife, who had been attracted by the noise of the struggle, started downstairs. I held the man and called to her, "See if that man has a gun in his pocket."

My wife ran down, and while I held him, she placed her hand in his right overcoat pocket and got hold of a gun. She said, "Yes, George, he has."

I said, "For God's sake, hold it." I then grappled with him and threw him over the telephone stand in the hall entrance. He released his hand from my grasp and, while my wife still held the gun, he pulled a knife from inside of his overcoat, a knife such as I never saw before.

It had a blade twelve to fourteen inches long. He cut across my right arm and got me. Then I fired at him. Then [Shippy's driver] Foley fired.

About this time, my boy, Harry, started downstairs after his mother. He cried, "Papa, I will help you."

Then I heard a shot entirely different from my gun and Foley's gun. I saw my wife was not able to keep up the unequal struggle. The assassin had wrenched the gun away from her. Then as my boy grappled with him,

Fig. 3. Chicago chief of police, George M. Shippy.

he shot Harry just above the heart. I saw Harry fall to the stairs. As he did so, he cried, "Papa, I'm shot; I can't help you anymore."

Then I shot to kill. I had only shot to disable before. But when my boy cried that he had been shot, I shot to kill. I put one bullet in that fellow's head and another through his heart.

> Afterward I found out that the fellow had fired a shot earlier than the one that hit my boy. The second shot fired by him went through Foley's right hand, causing him to drop his revolver.
>
> This was the third visit made to my house by this fellow. Sunday morning he had called after I had left for the city hall.
>
> Harry let this fellow in then. The man said he wanted to see the chief, and Harry answered, "My father has gone to work."
>
> This fellow came again this morning at 7 o'clock. The maid, Therese Tauer, informed him that he could not see me until 9 o'clock.
>
> He returned at the hour she had suggested and the shooting followed.

Even in the very newspapers that printed excerpts of Shippy's statement, it had been proved that the dead young man was not Sicilian or Armenian and that he seemed younger than Shippy's appraisal. None of the newspapers dared question the essence of the story, however: that the young man was an anarchist bent on assassinating Chief Shippy in his own home.

The Averbuch shooting was chilling enough news, but it took on even darker tones in the public mind because of two almost simultaneous, though minor, events. The evening before the shooting, two men were seen skulking around a prison where Captain P. D. O'Brien, commander of the detective bureau, was on duty. Although the men were quickly frightened off, one officer claimed he had seen one of the men reach toward his hip as if he were contemplating reaching for a gun. The next afternoon, in the light of the Averbuch shooting, the incident was being reported as an assassination attempt against O'Brien.

On the morning of the shooting, when Mayor Busse returned from visiting Shippy during his brief hospital stay, he was ac-

Sanguinary Struggle in the Residence of Chief Shippy.

Fig. 4. Newspaper account of the struggle.

costed by a shabbily dressed man described by newspapers as a crank. According to one account, the man said to Busse, "I want a job and I am not coming here to ask you for one anymore. If I don't get a position something is going to happen." Busse's response, "You have been here every day for four months," made clear he was familiar with the man, but most newspapers downplayed that angle. By late afternoon, the event was widely reported as an assassination attempt against Busse.

Fueled by Shippy's declaration that his attacker was an anarchist and the coincidence of other public officials being harassed,

Chicago's newspapers immediately sensed conspiracy. Some tried to attach the still unidentified Averbuch to the assassination on February 23 of Father Leo Heinrichs in Denver, Colorado. Others looked for links back to the killing of President McKinley in 1901. Father P. J. O'Calaghan of Chicago's St. Mary's Church, who delivered his Sunday sermon with two detectives standing guard, suggested a link between the Averbuch incident and the threats he had received himself.[14]

Among the Monday afternoon papers rushing into print with an incomplete story was the *Daily News*, already established as one of the city's leading papers. In restraint uncharacteristic of Chicago's journalism of the time, the paper referred to Shippy's victim only as a "supposed anarchist." Nevertheless, it reported in the first paragraph of its lead story, "The assassin is declared to have been an anarchist and may have been the leader of a plot aimed at others beside the chief." Later in its coverage, it described the actual shooting more dramatically even than Chief Shippy had. Reporting the climax of the event, it wrote:

> In the meantime, the assassin had drawn a knife, seven inches long and brand new with which he lunged at the Chief. Shippy dodged back, but received the full force of the blow in the right side, directly beneath the armpit. An artery was severed and the blood which gushed forward blinded Foley who was about to shoot the assassin. The anarchist turned and fired at the driver, shattering his right wrist.

The reporter mentions no source for the embellishments on Shippy's original account.

The *Daily Journal* was broader in its coverage. After releasing an extra edition, it devoted the entire front page of its Monday afternoon edition, except the leftmost column, to the killing. It

Fig. 5. Harry Shippy and driver James Foley.
Photograph: *Chicago Daily News.* Chicago Historical Society. DN–005952.

featured a large, three-column photo of Averbuch's face—puffed from recent death—at the center of the page, in its chief subhead it wrote, "Family Home Scene of Fiendish Attempt to Wreak Revenge for Activity Against Reds," and in its version of the gunfight it wrote:

When attacked at his door by a murderous stranger,
Chief Shippy sought only to disable his assailant. Even
after he had been terribly slashed under his right
shoulder by a knife he did not seek to slay. But when he
heard the moan of his wounded son saying, "Papa, I
am shot and can help you no more," he shot down the
stranger in his tracks with a bullet through his head
and another through the heart.

"When I was down and heard my poor boy say that
he was shot I never expected to see light another
minute. I felt that I was a goner. I heard the report of a
strange gun and gave up all hope," said the Chief.

Two columns away, also on the front page, was the text of the
statement Shippy had written in the several hours after the shooting. It would be some time before anyone wondered at the quick-
ness of Shippy's recovery from so serious a wound.

The *Daily Journal* also reported that a box of lozenges found
in the dead assassin's possession seemed to indicate he was from
Meadville in Crawford County. In addition, it claimed, the police had determined he was either an Italian or a Russian.

It was left to William Randolph Hearst's *Chicago Evening
American* to provide the most sensational coverage. With its characteristic double tier of screaming headlines, it issued three separate editions that Monday evening. It offered the claim that the
assassin had spied on Chief Shippy for the past ten days. It also
quoted Assistant Chief of Police Herman Schuettler with a new
explanation of the conspiracy theory:

"I believe the man was not only an anarchist," declared
Assistant Chief Schuettler, "but I believe that he was
selected by lot at a certain anarchists' meeting some
days ago to assassinate the chief. If my theories bear
out, I shall have his accomplices in custody soon."

In its final edition of the evening, it reported, correctly, that the assassin had lived on the West Side. It, too, ran the photo of Averbuch but left it unretouched, the bullet holes clearly visible. By the morning of Tuesday, March 4, when the next wave of newspapers came out, the police had determined that the man Shippy killed was Lazarus Averbuch, a Jew. Although little was known for certain about the recent immigrant, newspapers seized upon the identity as a resolution to the mystery of the assassination. A photograph of a living Lazarus Averbuch, taken from a postcard photo he had recently had made to send to his parents in Austria, became momentarily ubiquitous. The contents of his personal library—which featured nothing more indicative of his political views than *Living in Tents in Siberia, The People's Work: How the Social Democrats Look on the Peasantry and the Land Question, What the Constitution Teaches,* and *Stories from Russian History*—were front-page news. Still, no one in the mainstream press questioned Shippy's assertions that his attacker was an anarchist.

The *Record-Herald*, which claimed to have the largest circulation of any two-cent newspaper in the city (that is, larger than any paper other than Hearst's one-cent *Evening American*), wrote of the shooting as if the affair were entirely closed. A box atop the front page provided the essentials of the incident:

The Place	Chief Shippy's Home
The Time	8:30 A.M.
Slain Assassin	Harry Averbuch [*sic*]
The Motive	Defiance of Law

After claiming that Averbuch fought "with all the maddened fury of a fiend incarnate," it went on to explain the motive for the crime more fully:

DEATH STRUGGLE WON BY SHIPPY.

Chief of Police, Wounded by Assassin's Knife, Tells of Fierce Battle.

SON AND EMPLOYE SHOT.

Boy Wounded in Lung and Driver's Hand Injured Before Assailant Is Killed.

The fears of police officials, expressed in THE TRIBUNE several days ago, that their lives were in danger were realized yesterday when an avowed anarchist, Lazarus Averbuch, tried to assassinate Chief Shippy of the police department, and was himself slain.

The tragic attempt on the life of the chief and the killing of the anarchist occurred in the front hallway of the chief's residence, 31 Lincoln place—near North Clark street and Webster avenue.

It was just after 9 o'clock when the man appeared and the tragic incidents followed quickly. The results were:

Chief Shippy, stabbed under his arm, the wound being slight.

The chief's son, Henry, was shot through the lung, above the heart, but probably will recover.

Chief Shippy's driver, Foley, shot through the hand.

The anarchist assailant, shot dead.

Attempt on Sunday Foiled.

It is evident that the young anarchist meant to kill the chief on Sunday. All of that day Shippy was in touch with the reports being made by the detectives detailed to guard Roman Catholic churches from possible anarchist attacks. He went down to his office once and spent considerable time in the North Halsted street police station, in which precinct he lives. At noon all the reports were in and showed no attempts at violence. The chief returned to his Sunday dinner relieved of much apprehension.

Figs. 6 and 7. Newspaper accounts citing anarchy.

SHIPPY'S SHOT ANARCHY'S KNELL

EXTRA

WOULD-BE SLAYER A RUSSIAN 'RED.'

Police Identify Man Who Tried to Murder Shippy as Lazarus Averbuch.

NEWCOMER FROM KISHENEFF

He Was Engaged Saturday Distributing Circulars for Emma Goldman Meeting.

MARCHER WITH DR. REITMAN.

THE ASSASSIN.

Name... Lazarus (Harry) Averbuch
Age... 20 years
Nationality... Russian Jew
Birthplace... Kisheneff

Outraged People Demand Swift Punishment and New and Drastic Laws.

COUNT ON COUNCIL'S AID.

Yesterday's Crime Expected to Lead to More Stringent Rules Against Alien "Undesirables."

BAR TO INCENDIARY SPEECHES.

> [The assassination attempt] is linked with the slaying
> of Father Leo Heinrichs at Denver, February 23, while
> the priest was administering holy communion at the
> altar rail of his church to Giuseppe Alio [*sic*], his slayer,
> and it is the direct outcome of a remarkable subterra-
> nean growth of anarchism in Chicago, of which the
> police have been cognizant for nearly a year past and to
> stop which they have recently adopted drastic rem-
> edies.
>
> In retaliation for his activities toward the suppres-
> sion of the reds, Chief Shippy is supposed to have been
> picked as the first victim.

The *Tribune*, already long established as a major paper in the city,
was bolder in its claims. Making the connection, as had The *Daily
Journal*, between the incident and the imminent arrival of Emma
Goldman, the country's most noted anarchist speaker, it concluded there was a clear plot against government in Chicago:

> Averbuch was an anarchist of a morbid, insane type, a
> disciple of Emma Goldman, "Queen of the Reds," and
> probably a marcher in the recent parade of the unem-
> ployed which had "Dr." Ben Reitman at its head. He
> was inspired to his murderous attack upon the chief of
> police partly by the rebuff which the marchers received
> at the hands of the police and partly by the announce-
> ment of the police department that Miss Goldman
> would not be allowed to speak on anarchy at German
> Hod Carriers hall next Friday, as was scheduled.

The *Tribune* also came forward with the theory that Averbuch
had not been operating alone. Rather, he had an unidentified
accomplice, a young man with whom he had been studying the
last several weeks. It reported, "It is believed the young anarchist
had a partner in his work who thus far is only known as the curly-

Fig. 8. Averbuch portrayed as anarchist.

haired boy." At the top of the page was the photo of the young Averbuch flanked by one picture of a fist clenching a long dagger, another of a pistol, and a bomb drawn between the weapons.

The shooting worried not just Chicago, but all the country. The *New York Times* made news of the killing its lead story. Although the general tone of its reporting was subdued in comparison to that in the Chicago papers, it nonetheless reported information that later proved untrue. Making a similar connection between Goldman's speaking and the incident, it wrote:

> The assailant was tonight identified as Lazarus
> Averbuch, an avowed anarchist and follower of Emma

Goldman. On Saturday, he distributed copies of a
circular advertising an address by Emma Goldman in
Chicago on March 6. The circular was headed: "Long
live those who fight for liberty."

Not even the *Times* could entirely avoid waxing dramatic in its
writing of the event. It wrote further:

The assassin apparently had dressed himself for death.
He wore black clothes and overcoat, a new hat, and
clean linen, all of fairly good quality. He had been
freshly shaved, and his hair had been trimmed recently.

Although the case would remain front-page news for another two
weeks almost without interruption, the essentials of what
Chief Shippy had said took place that morning remained the
official story. The name of Averbuch was, to the mass of Chicago's
populace, synonymous with anarchy, communism, malevolent
foreigners, and violence. Most people did not yet know that he
was a spottily educated, small, nineteen-year-old boy somewhat
overwhelmed by the strange country in which he found himself living.

One reason for the hysteria over the shooting was that it raised
the specter of a second Haymarket Square incident. Although the
original Haymarket incident had taken place nearly a quarter century before, it remained a source of anxiety to the city. Many of
Shippy's officers had been on the force the day an unknown person threw the bomb that killed several of their colleagues. Seven
labor organizers, so-called anarchists, were arrested, tried, and
sentenced to death. Three were actually hung; a fourth died in
his cell from what was proclaimed a suicide. The case had been
reopened in 1892 by then Illinois governor John Altgeld. He found

there had been a miscarriage of justice in the trial and pardoned the remaining three prisoners. When he was defeated for reelection four years later, his Haymarket decision was seen as a prime reason for his decline in popularity.[15]

The Haymarket Affair did not entirely die down. The city constructed a large monument on the site to honor the murdered police officers, and anarchists responded by turning the graves of the executed leaders into a national shrine for left-wing activism. To some it was an example of what could happen when law enforcement permitted radical agitation, while to others it was a clear-cut instance of government abuse. To many others it loomed as a near insurrection.

Slight as the parallels were, then, with Lazarus Averbuch's having been killed in George Shippy's house, they were sufficient to alarm the city even beyond the specter of a ring of assassins looking to kill prominent local citizens. The *Record-Herald* reported:

> The police point out a great and dangerous difference between the anarchists of the Haymarket riot days and those of today. In 1886 the "reds" tried to inflame their followers against the authorities in general. They picked out no individuals. In these days, however, they are specialists in their harangues and incitements.

The Daily Journal, as part of its extensive coverage of the incident, interviewed a number of public and clerical officials on their reactions. It quoted State Representative John J. Poulton:

> The enemies of this government should be cleaned out, sent from this city and from this country. The American people will never tolerate the assassin's knife as a means of protest or a means of curing real or fancied evils.

It quoted Reverend George L. Robinson, head of the McCormick Theological Seminary:

> The people of Chicago are more badly frightened now than at any time since the Haymarket riot. We must do something to put an end to this lawlessness. When people cannot obey the laws of this country, then something should be done to compel them.

State's Attorney J. J. Healy—the same man preparing the case against Shippy for his alleged protection of the Mont Tennes gambling concession—spoke to the *Daily News* about the parallels he saw between the incidents. "If any evidence develops that shows that this attack was made by an anarchist," he said, "grand jury action will be taken. The inquiry will not stop with the tools which attempt the assassination, but will go back to the instigators. The example of the Haymarket riot will be followed and we will go back to the men who are really responsible, to the agitators."

Although direct talk of the Haymarket parallels soon quieted, the mere surfacing of such a connection made it difficult to address the Averbuch situation coolly. Just as the specter of the 1871 Paris Commune had frightened Americans at the time of the Haymarket explosion, so recollections of the Haymarket incident cast a heavy pall over the reaction of Chicago's media to the event that occurred on March 3, 1908.

As a consequence of such tensions, labeling Lazarus Averbuch an anarchist had great appeal at such a moment. As someone whose front-page photo recalled the faces of any number of Russian, Italian, or Jewish immigrants, Averbuch served immediately as a symbol of the foreigner. In a country still dedicated to the principle of open immigration, most newspaper commentators, politicians, and other government officials were reluctant to demonstrate any public fear or hatred of the strange, funny-sounding immigrants swelling the city, but they could condemn anarchists. Averbuch the anarchist was also Averbuch the foreigner. Suddenly, xenophobia had a focus. Averbuch had a name, nationality, and crime. Although events in the days following the shooting would seriously undermine the official story, much of the city refused to acknowledge any new version; the version people found in these first hours was very much the one they wanted to believe. Averbuch the foreigner should not have come to the city in the first place.

Jane Addams, of Chicago's Hull House, the best known of Chicago's settlement houses, saw that part of her role was to soothe tensions between the established community and the new immigrants. From the vantage of someone who had been involved in the Averbuch Affair, she wrote some months later of the unfortunate backlash the immigrant community suffered as a result of the shooting:

> In fact, the more excited and irrational public opinion is, the more recklessly newspapers state mere surmises as facts and upon these surmises arouse unsubstantiated prejudices against certain immigrants, the more necessary it is that some body of people should be ready to put forward the spiritual and intellectual conditions of the foreign colony which is thus being made the subject of inaccurate surmises and unjust suspicion.[16]

Despite the best efforts of Addams and many others, those surmises and suspicions remained firmly in place in the days immediately following Averbuch's death. To most of the public, Lazarus Averbuch was a semi-crazed anarchist bent on killing Chief Shippy and his family for vague political reasons. But to the Jews of the West Side ghetto, it caused profound fear and consternation as the media stressed that the "anarchist" assassin was not Sicilian or Armenian, as Shippy first thought, but in fact was a newly arrived immigrant Jew. As some of the newest and least secure of Chicago's immigrants, the West Side Jews had every reason to fear a new wave of xenophobia.

III

THE POLICE IN ACTION

March 3–6

Among the groups to whom the Averbuch Affair remained a real and changing concern was the police department. Even as the newspapers gave the public a story it found fascinating, the police were at work tracking down Averbuch's friends and acquaintances, investigating any activity that smacked lightly of anarchism, and advocating legislation against political speech. Although many of their leads came to naught, the police were astonishingly busy in the first seventy-two hours after the shooting.

Chief Shippy himself took almost no part in the investigation. Exactly why he was debilitated is not clear, but there are a number of possible explanations. First, he had been wounded in the scuffle with Averbuch. Reports on the nature of his injuries varied, and a few sources claim he was seriously hurt. Although his being hale enough to file a written report within hours of the incident suggests he could not have been too seriously injured, it is possible he remained off the case to give himself time to heal.

Second, he would also have been understandably concerned about his son. Harry Shippy was reported by some accounts to be near death for the few days immediately following the shooting; Shippy may well have held back from the investigation to be with his son. The third possibility, however, is that the department simply held Shippy off the case. It might have considered him too involved in the affair to lead a competent investigation or, possibly, have recognized in him an instability that it no longer trusted with complete authority.

In any event, the mantle of leadership in the department passed to Herman Scheuttler, the police force's consummate insider. A twenty-five-year veteran of the force who had served through the Haymarket Affair, Scheuttler had been an assistant general superintendent for five years. He had earned some notoriety for solving the Louisa Luetgert murder case in 1897—in which Adolph Luetgert, the owner of a sausage manufacturing company, had disposed of his wife's body by throwing her into his sausage grinder—but wielded most of his influence behind the scenes.[17] Given his first opportunity to direct the entire force, he took over with relish.

Scheuttler's first task was to identify Averbuch. He put an unprecedented three thousand officers on alert, a group the *Inter Ocean* called the "biggest 'dragnet' ever thrown out in Chicago." Acting under the unquestioned presumption that the would-be assassin was an anarchist, he had his men search anarchist gathering places and raid publishing houses for information. He went so far as to create a special anarchist squad, composed of three detectives.

When one member of the force, Detective Sergeant "Make" Mills, announced he was certain he had seen the dead man at the recent March of the Unemployed led by Ben Reitman, the police began looking for Reitman. Before they could find him, he arrived at the morgue of his own accord. Asked whether he could identify the body, Reitman shook his head. "I don't know whether this fellow was an anarchist or not," he said. "I know he wasn't a hobo. I thought I knew most of the cranks in Chicago, but I never knew this man."[18]

Turning to the leading investigative methods of the day, the police asked several physicians to analyze the body for physical attributes that would shed light on the dead man's character. Dr. Otto W. Lewke, one of the examiners, declared that Averbuch, "according to the theories of criminologists, was a degenerate."[19] Peter Hoffman, the coroner conducting the autopsy, determined that Averbuch's cranium was of a "peculiar formation," and designated doctors Warren Hunter and Harold Moyer to examine Averbuch's brain for signs of insanity or imbalance.[20] The *Daily News* ran a diagram identifying various features of his face and skull that marked him as the "anarchist type."

The hostility many officers felt toward Averbuch and anarchists in general was made clear during the evening Averbuch's body was left open at the morgue. The body lay naked on a viewing table and anyone was free to look at it for purposes of making an identification or simply out of curiosity. Scheuttler, apparently, encouraged his officers to view the body. According to the *Chicago Daily Socialist*, whose correspondent remained in the examining room throughout the evening, many police officers insulted the corpse or made hostile gestures toward it. One officer went so far as to walk up to Averbuch's body and strike it in the face. No one, according to the correspondent, raised any objections to the act.

The police thought they had identified the body for a brief moment just hours after the shooting. A saloonkeeper named Mary Adams came forward claiming that she recognized the man from his pictures in the newspapers. She said she was nearly

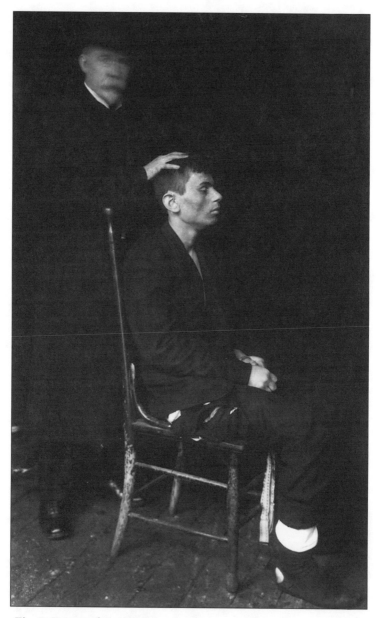

Fig. 9. Deceased Lazarus Averbuch.
Photograph: *Chicago Daily News.* Chicago Historical Society. DN–005897.

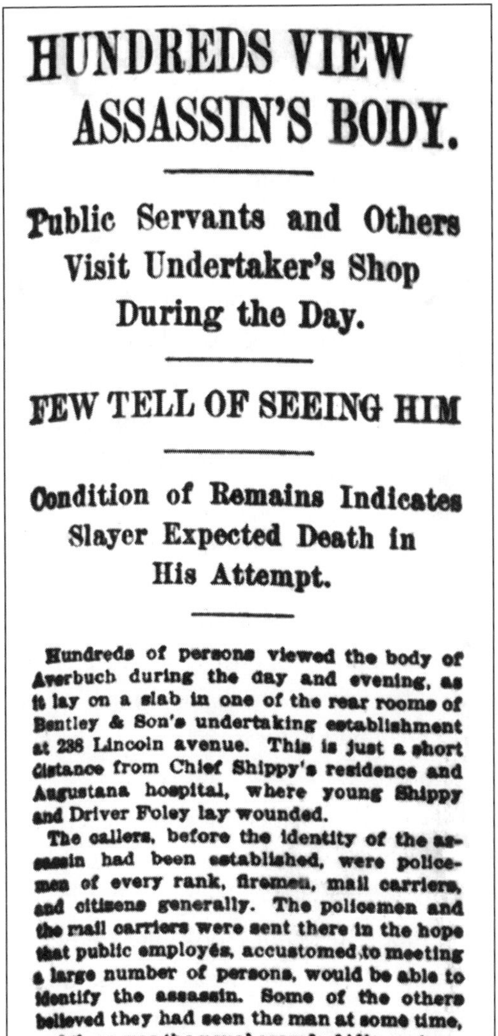

HUNDREDS VIEW ASSASSIN'S BODY.

Public Servants and Others Visit Undertaker's Shop During the Day.

FEW TELL OF SEEING HIM

Condition of Remains Indicates Slayer Expected Death in His Attempt.

Hundreds of persons viewed the body of Averbuch during the day and evening, as it lay on a slab in one of the rear rooms of Bentley & Son's undertaking establishment at 238 Lincoln avenue. This is just a short distance from Chief Shippy's residence and Augustana hospital, where young Shippy and Driver Foley lay wounded.

The callers, before the identity of the assassin had been established, were policemen of every rank, firemen, mail carriers, and citizens generally. The policemen and the mail carriers were sent there in the hope that public employés, accustomed to meeting a large number of persons, would be able to identify the assassin. Some of the others believed they had seen the man at some time, and there was the usual crowd of idly curious.

From the talk of some of the visitors, it was found that the man had been hanging around the neighborhood for days. He had asked for the residence of Chief Shippy.

Fig. 10. Newspaper account of body.

certain his name was Adams (although he was not a relative of hers) and that he had briefly tended bar for her. She further claimed that he had frequented a club at 85 W. Fifteenth Street.

Even as they were trying to confirm that initial identification, yet another person came forward to say he recognized the face that was now on virtually every front page in the city. R. M. Miller, a fellow employee of Averbuch's at Eichengreen's egg-packing company, reported to the police that he thought the man might be Averbuch. Beyond the resemblance, Miller said, was the unusual fact that Averbuch had not come to work that day. According to the *Inter Ocean*'s Tuesday morning edition, Miller also described Averbuch as a vicious anarchist. The *Inter Ocean* continued, without attribution, to report that Averbuch had been heard to grow angry at police attempts to prevent Emma Goldman from speaking. He had been heard to cry aloud, "Chief Shippy ought to be killed for refusing to permit Emma Goldman to speak." The same report mentioned as fact that "almost every book in [Averbuch's] flat was on socialism or anarchy, and the wrongs of the poor. Thirty odd volumes on these subjects were confiscated by the police."

Acting on the tentative identification, Scheuttler had his men arrest Olga Averbuch and conduct a thorough search of the Averbuchs' tiny apartment. Using what the *Daily News* called "Sweatbox Methods," the police took Olga to the morgue's viewing room without warning her what she would find there. They planned, it seems, to shock out of her some admission of her brother's involvement with anarchist groups. On seeing Lazarus's body, however, she grew hysterical. She screamed in recognition, wailed against her brother's death, and eventually fainted.

Hoping still to get information out of her, the police kept her in custody at the station the remainder of that night and into the next evening. They questioned her repeatedly about Lazarus's history, interests, and recent movements. They followed every thread they could imagine that might connect him to an anarchist plot, grilling her about his acquaintances and affiliations. When she could tell them of no such plot, they brought in W. H. Eichengreen, who had been her own benefactor before employing her brother, to try to ply the story from her. She denied yet again that there was any story to tell. Her brother had been frustrated at not being able to find work, she claimed, but he was not a student of anarchist thought nor was he in any way prone to violence.

Although the police could take no direct clues from Olga's testimony, they nonetheless continued on the assumption that Averbuch had been an anarchist. They did learn from Olga that he had recently been friends with a "curly-haired" young man. From neighbors they heard rumors that Olga's friend and recent boarder, Rosie Stern, was Lazarus's sweetheart. And from simple conjecture they figured that he must somehow have been connected to a group of Chicago Jewish anarchists, identified as the Edelstadt Group, named in memory of a brilliant Yiddish anarchist poet who had died at a young age a few years earlier. On the strength of such evidence, they launched manhunts for the "curly-haired" young man, Rosie Stern, and a young Edelstadt member, Harry Goldstein.

It is difficult to tell exactly how many other people were arrested in the first few days after the shooting. Several, including the unfortunate Mary Adams, whose initial identification of the body proved false, were held for little apparent reason and then released after several hours or maybe a day. One pair, Edward Berman and William Siegal, were held for a couple of days when an ambiguous message between them, "The game is up. Get out of town quick," was intercepted. Because Berman was labeled an anarchist, perhaps by his own admission, perhaps by accusation, the two were assumed to have some connection to the Averbuch case. Joseph Freedman, a self-professed anarchist, was arrested for declaring on a public bus that he wished Shippy had been killed.

The first arrest police made that had any genuine connection to Averbuch, after the arrest of Olga, came when they discovered Isadore Maron, a young friend of Averbuch's, dropping by the Washburne apartment to look for his friend the morning following the shooting. Maron was originally arrested on the assumption that he was the "curly-haired" accomplice, but his thick, straight hair made clear he could not have been. He said he was a friend of Averbuch's and that the two had gone to a political meeting together. It was only a single meeting, he insisted, one that was convened to make plans for a restaurant that would serve food to some of the city's hungry. He further told police that Rosie Stern no longer lived with the Averbuchs but that he didn't know her new address. Otherwise, he had no information for the authorities. Nevertheless, he was held in custody for several days.

Early in the afternoon of the same day, Monday, March 3, police caught up with Harry Goldstein. As secretary of the Edelstadt Group, Goldstein was a committed anarchist, but he claimed to know nothing of Averbuch or any assassination plot.[21] He was considered a witness of such significance that Mayor Busse himself came to the police station to interrogate him. Police refused to disclose information about their questioning of him, but it seems clear they ultimately learned nothing. Because Goldstein had a full head of curly hair, he was quickly labeled the "curly-haired" youth who was Averbuch's friend. Since he quickly proved he didn't know Averbuch at all, the case against him was dropped. He, too, however, was imprisoned for several days.

In the thirty-six hours following the shooting, the newspapers managed to turn the search for Rosie Stern into a cause

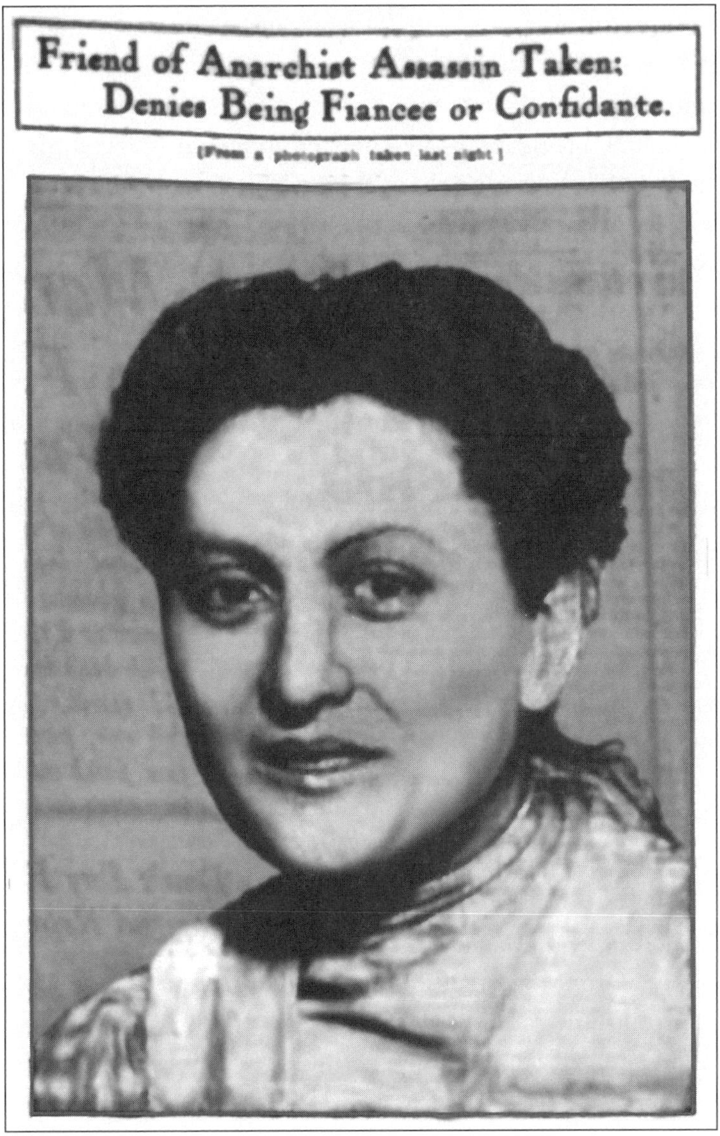

Friend of Anarchist Assassin Taken; Denies Being Fiancee or Confidante.

[From a photograph taken last night]

Fig. 11. Rosa Stern.

célèbre. Scheuttler was quoted as saying he hoped her arrest would make clear the entire story of the affair, and the *Evening American* called her the "pretty anarchist queen sweetheart of Averbuch." Although one paper printed police suppositions that she had fled to Milwaukee and the tone of most reports made her out to be a public enemy, she actually proved just to be at work. Not having read any newspapers either on the Monday of the shooting or the Tuesday following, Stern had no idea she was wanted and went to her work as a seamstress at Beifield's Tailoring on 324 W. Adams Street.

Once they took her into custody, the police were determined to pull a story from her. They "sweated" her all afternoon, but learned nothing. She claimed to be Olga's friend, not Lazarus's, and that she knew absolutely nothing of his affairs. As Scheuttler paraded one arrestee in after another, trying to trap her in some spark of recognition, she maintained she knew no one the police were trying to connect to the case. Undaunted, he had her held in the same prison as Olga. He made certain, however, that Olga did not learn of the arrest. The *Inter Ocean* speculated he feared Olga would draw strength from her friend's resistance.

Despite getting virtually nowhere with the prisoners they held, the police continued pursuing the anarchist-assassin theory. Operating on the presumption that the whole affair would be clear if only one suspect could be made to talk, they held Olga Averbuch, Stern, Maron, Goldstein, and several others against what would seem due process. It would take several days before any commentators pointed out the irony that the police, in fighting against anarchy, were recklessly disregarding the law themselves.

Many members of the police department, apparently including both Shippy and Scheuttler, believed the Averbuch case was actually just a skirmish in what they took to be an imminent war against anarchy. As important as it was to them to solve the Averbuch case, they were simultaneously determined to attack organized anarchy. To that end, they took the lead in proposing restrictions on free speech and the circulation of anarchist writings, calling on the government to approve laws permitting the deportation of anyone linked to anarchism, and urging limits on immigrants who were likely to carry or be influenced by anarchistic thought. Most directly, they determined they would not permit Emma Goldman, the noted anarchist, to speak anywhere in the city under any circumstances, despite her announcement, long before the Averbuch case broke, of her intention to make a speaking tour in the Midwest, including Chicago.

The department took it almost as a duty to shut down political speech it decided was potentially subversive. Scheuttler and Inspector Wheeler, commander of the 1st Police Division, held a conference announcing a new crackdown on any and all anarchists. According to the *Daily News*, Wheeler said the force would arrest or drive from Chicago any anarchists of whom the force was aware. "This city is fast approaching the point where it was at the time of the Haymarket Riot, as far as disturbers are concerned," he said. "And we will bring them all in—Russian, Italian, or any other nationality."[22] When Mayor Busse began discussing his own plans to drive anarchy from the city, he met with wide approval. According to the *Inter Ocean*, "The aldermen are unanimous in their desire to stamp out anarchy, and all express themselves as willing to support any administration measure."

In a similar vein, Busse came out in favor of banning all street meetings. His administration hoped thereby to prevent the sorts of gatherings that erupted into the Haymarket Riot. In instituting such a law, however, the city would therefore have made it illegal for the Salvation Army, among other groups, to continue operating. An unidentified aide to Busse told the *Daily News*, "Every crank and fanatic in Chicago may now get up in a public street and decry our form of popular government and it is time that a stop is put to it. . . . The men who are not satisfied with our government should get out of the country."

Moving from the local to the federal scene, Busse and Scheuttler, among others, held a press conference to announce a national strategy against anarchy. A Chicago task force, to be headed by Chief Shippy, would work not simply to drive anarchists from the city but to see they were deported as well. United States Attorney General Charles Bonaparte pledged federal support for anti-anarchist efforts if necessary, while Oscar Straus, Roosevelt's secretary of commerce and labor, announced plans to extend provisions for deporting anarchists. The law in 1907 made it possible to deport anyone engaged in anarchist activities who had arrived in the country less than three years earlier. A lead article contained in the *New York Times* on March 4 outlined Straus's orders to federal immigration authorities to cooperate with local police in "putting down terrorism." At the local level, Illinois State's Attorney Healy (the man conducting the investigations against Busse and Shippy) virtually ceded direction of the anti-anarchist campaign to Shippy, saying, "I shall be guided largely in anything I may do by what the police decide is best. Chief Shippy knows the situation far better than I do." The point of the new strategy, different from the old only in scope, was to push anarchists as far away as possible from Chicago.

On the very day of Averbuch's death, Representative Adolph J. Sabath, from Chicago, was speaking in Washington, D.C., in opposition to attempts to broaden existing laws that would make it easier to deport aliens. The Averbuch case was immediately seized upon by the federal administration to gain support for stricter immigration laws.

While Scheuttler and his men found nothing of substance in the Averbuch investigation and considered different strategies to combat known anarchists, the police had a tangible distraction readying herself to come to Chicago. With the shooting, Emma

Goldman's tour became a focal point for the anti-anarchist hysteria that the police and press were fanning. As the best-known revolutionary speaker in the United States, and quite possibly in the world, Goldman's visits sparked controversy everywhere. Initially, neither Scheuttler nor Busse came forward announcing that she would not be permitted to speak, but Scheuttler did announce the cancelation of her first scheduled talk for the night of Friday, March 6.

In the meantime, Chicago police received word from their St. Louis counterparts that Goldman had left for Chicago on or before March 4. Assuming she had already arrived by March 5, Scheuttler's men searched more than twenty-five homes on the West Side in the "anarchist colony" where Goldman stayed when she visited the city in 1901. The police were instructed to arrest her on sight, despite the fact that they had no warrant. Eventually Scheuttler notified the entire department to be on the alert for her, but no one could discover any sign of her until days later.

Chicago's police were at an anxious impasse. Publicly they maintained the Averbuch investigation was proceeding well. Privately, they must certainly have been shaken by their ultimate inability to connect Averbuch with any substantial anarchist groups. In three days of "sweating" Olga Averbuch and Lazarus's other friends, they were unable to put together any acceptable theory or even to develop any promising leads. Why Averbuch had gone to Shippy's home was a greater mystery than ever, and the police decided to confront that mystery by ignoring it. Busse's, Shippy's, and Scheuttler's stepped-up anti-anarchism campaign seems in retrospect to have been calculated in part to deflect attention away from the Averbuch incident. Unable to crack the mystery that touched their own department, they raised the stakes of the affair and took on the specter of international anarchy and the real but slippery presence of Emma Goldman.

IV

THE USUAL SUSPECTS

STIRRINGS ON THE LEFT WING

March 3–6

Although it is apparent that Busse, Scheuttler, and Straus had good reasons to exaggerate the threat of left-wing groups in Chicago and across the country, they did not fabricate the existence of such groups. The first decade of the century may not have been the watershed period of social and labor agitation that the 1880s had been or the 1910s or 1930s would be, but it did see considerable organization outside traditional American politics.[23] As a result, there were organizations and publications threatened by and compelled to respond to the stepped-up pressure of the new anti-anarchism campaign. It took several days before these dissenting voices made themselves heard, but from the moment of Averbuch's killing they found themselves in a new, even less tolerant Chicago.

It should not be surprising that a society as diverse as the Chicago of 1908, confronted as it was by colossal unemployment and masses of immigrants unsure of their roles in the new country, sought a wide variety of social solutions. Many of those immigrants were steeped in the incipient socialism of Leo Tolstoy, Peter Kropotkin, and Michael Bakunin, and they took to preaching one variety of socialism or another as a cure to the troubles of contemporary life. Some went no further than to circulate handbills or decry capitalism from corners of streets in the ghetto or neighboring areas. Others established study or action groups, or worked for publications like the *Daily Socialist* or any of the many other foreign language or socialist newspapers.

Louis Post, publisher of the *Public*, was only one of the many socialist-inspired thinkers in the city. Although his magazine never achieved wide circulation, it remained remarkably influential. Post himself was a lawyer, author of several books, and a successful Chicago lecturer. He was an intellectual before he was an activist and made a name for himself as a proponent of the single tax first proposed by the economist Henry George. As a publisher and chief writer, though, he found himself embroiled in many of Chicago's social questions. A sometime politician, he reached the zenith of his career when Woodrow Wilson appointed him assistant secretary for the Department of Labor.[24]

Chicago remained a center for organized labor, as well. It had been the site of the Knights of Labor's worst conflicts in the 1880s, particularly the strike at Cyrus McCormick's Reaper Works that precipitated the fateful Haymarket Square protest. In the Pullman Strike of 1894, Chicago saw the most bitterly fought labor battle of its history. The American Railroad Union, led by future presidential candidate Eugene Debs, struck against the virtually totalitarian conditions imposed by George Pullman in the company town that bore his name. Although the strike was eventually broken with federal assistance, it remained an unhealed wound throughout the early years of the century.

From the ruins of the Pullman Strike, a number of unions that suffered in their support of Debs's union managed to rebuild. Originally under the leadership of the corrupt Skinny Madden and later the reformer John Fitzpatrick, the Chicago Federation of Labor proved itself one of the most substantial of the many fledgling labor federations in the country. Representing several different skilled trades, it helped pave the way for the coming of modern unionism to Chicago. In 1908, three years after the success of Fitzpatrick's reform candidacy, the federation helped stamp Chicago as a city very much alive to the labor question.[25]

Chicago was also a center of the settlement house movement that thrived throughout the country from the late 1880s until World War II. The most famous of the settlement houses in the city was Hull House. There future Nobel Laureate Jane Addams and her coterie of social workers worked to interpret American culture to immigrants from all parts of the world and, against greater odds, to explain to the world of George Shippy and Fred Busse the conditions and mindsets of the newly arrived Americans. Addams saw her mission extending beyond social work, and she took an active role in partisan politics and urban administration. Whether it was negotiating between the Pullman strikers and their management or seeing that her West Side neighbors received proper garbage collection service, she threw herself into controversial issue after controversial issue whenever she felt social justice was on the line.[26]

Chicago boasted more than one prominent settlement house. A scarce mile and a half north of Hull House was Chicago Commons, directed by theologian and activist Charles Taylor. Like Addams, Taylor frequently found himself allied with the underprivileged against a society that did not entirely understand them. Farther south, in Packingtown, Mary McDowell oversaw the operation of the University of Chicago Settlement House. An early worker with Addams at Hull House, McDowell was especially active in the Pullman Strike and in subsequent efforts to enact national child labor legislation.[27]

Among Chicago's other left-wing characters was the uncategorizeable Ben Reitman. By training a physician and by temperament a hobo, Reitman worked to alleviate the lots of both kinds of "tramps," the unemployed by choice and the unemployed by circumstance. As founder and chief operator of Chicago's Hobo College, he eventually won the title "King of the Hobos"—a title he may have bestowed upon himself. On May 31, 1907, Reitman held a "sociological clinic," to which he invited socialites to hear twenty-five hobos speak of their experiences.[28] Perhaps with that success in mind, or perhaps driven by his seeming urge for notoriety, he later took charge of the March of the Unemployed on January 23, 1908. It was at that march, subsequently broken up by the police, who also beat and arrested Reitman, that detectives claimed to have spotted the otherwise unknown Lazarus Averbuch.

Among all the groups concerned with social justice, though, Schuettler, Busse, and Straus singled out for attention the anarchists. The very word *anarchy* seemed to strike at the heart of what America stood for. With its laws and its call to public duty, America had brought order to a chaotic continent and a patchwork citizenry drawn from across the world. The media seized on such implications of anarchy and hammered home to the public the connection between anarchy and absolute lawlessness. On March 3, Bradley, the *Daily News*'s political cartoonist, depicted anarchists as wild-eyed, shadowy figures inhabiting a shrouded place called "Anarchy Alley." In its news section, the newspaper went on to explain that some anarchists urged people to open rebellion against government, but that "Other groups of anarchists direct their attention principally to attacking the present constitution of the home. The marriage ties in these groups are supplanted by doctrines of free love and the child in the home is taught not to respect the authority of anyone, not even the parents." Even the sober *Inter Ocean* wrote on March 4, "Orders went out from Washington to take the first step in purging the nation of these foes to government and individual life."

Much of the public accepted perceptions of anarchism in large part because of the violence adopted by some factions of the anarchist movement. Russian anarchists were responsible for assassinating numerous local and petty officials. In Portugal, in February 1908, anarchists had killed King Carlos and his heir. And, most chillingly for many Americans, an anarchist had killed President McKinley in 1901. Equally disturbing were the many reports of anarchist threats. Just a month before Averbuch was killed, an anarchist had shot and killed Father Leo Heinrichs, a Denver priest, and throughout the investigation of the Averbuch Affair, Chicago's newspapers would publish quoted threats and hints of threats against public officials and prominent religious figures.

Theoretical anarchism, though, was about a great deal more than political killing. A cousin to modern libertarianism, its view was that government was responsible for more ills than it relieved. The crux of its criticism was that government, by treating the interests of many separate individuals as a single corporate interest, intrinsically dehumanized its citizenry. In place of government, anarchy advocated elevating the contract between individuals. In such a way, the theory went, individuals would be involved only in those relationships they willingly entered into. Events such as wars and police brutality against the working class would therefore be impossible because individuals would never willingly hurt one another without individual provocation.

The motivation for anarchism was no different than the motivation for any social reform theory. Anarchist thinkers like

Russia's Michael Bakunin or France's Pierre Joseph Proudhon were generally, like Karl Marx, members of the upper class or the skilled labor class who came frequently into contact with the starving masses of unskilled laborers and the families they supported or, often, failed to support. To the media and public, there often seemed little difference between the anarchists and the socialists. Bakunin had, after all, joined Marx and Engels in the first Internationale. Adherents of both groups were routinely labeled "Reds."

One crucial difference between the two groups in 1908, however, was the comparative success of the movements they supported. Just as socialism was rebounding from the failure of the Russian Revolution of 1905 and was preparing for its greatest triumph in the Marxist Russian Revolution of 1917, anarchism was fading in influence. Anarchist theory had fueled the failed Paris Commune in 1871. In the United States, it had reached its highwater mark in 1886, when Albert Parsons and August Spies, labor leaders with strong anarchist influences, convened the Haymarket Square gathering in part to commemorate the Paris Commune. With their executions, anarchism never again spurred a broad-based movement in the United States.

Anarchist groups continued to operate nonetheless. Of those established in Chicago, the Edelstadt Group, composed of Jewish members, appears to have been the most successful by 1908. Named in honor of the dead Yiddish poet David Edelstadt and founded by his brother, it had an undeniable respectability to it that other, exclusively working class groups did not. In Chicago, its leaders were Miriam Yampolsky, a physician, and William Nathanson, a writer and philosopher, who later married one another. Yampolsky, described in the press as a "beautiful Jewess," was an early advocate of birth control and an effective figure for the group. She and Nathanson enjoyed an open marriage in that they lived separately at times, a situation that confounded the media and police. Yampolsky was a friend of Emma Goldman; the two corresponded, and Goldman stayed in Yampolsky's apartment on at least one of her visits to Chicago.[29] Neither Yampolsky nor Nathanson was arrested in the sweep made by Schuettler's forces, although Yampolsky in particular was the object of their surveillance. Instead, Schuettler's men arrested the group's treasurer, Harry Goldstein. Young, unemployed, and fairly well educated, he supported himself by selling anarchist pamphlets on the street. There is no evidence Goldstein ever met Averbuch, but—mostly because he had curly hair, like Averbuch's supposed accomplice—he was interrogated by a number of officers and held for several days.

Another prominent Chicago anarchist was Lucy Parsons. The widow of Albert Parsons, who had been executed for his part in organizing the Haymarket Square demonstration, she saw herself carrying the banner of the decapitated movement. As a frequent speaker at Hull House and Chicago Commons, she was under routine police surveillance.

The most influential anarchist in Chicago, however, did not actually live in the city at all. Emma Goldman had not been to Chicago since 1901, but she was universally recognized by Chicago anarchists as the movement's leading light. (It is an interesting historical footnote that Goldman claimed to have been converted to anarchy as a result of a Chicago incident: the execution of the Haymarket leaders.)[30] Although she had had some hand in assisting her friend Alexander Berkman in his attempted assassination of industrialist Henry Frick in 1902, Goldman insisted on the possibilities for anarchist action without violence.

Averbuch's killing took place a scant four days before Goldman was to arrive in Chicago for a series of fourteen public meetings. Police had tried to link Averbuch with posting fliers for her different speeches. It seems likely Shippy was nervous about increased anarchist activity precisely because of Goldman's arrival. He had forbidden her to speak in Chicago, and the initial police theory about Averbuch's motive for the perceived assassination attempt was that he wanted to take revenge on the chief for his prohibition of Goldman. Although police were never able to establish any link between Goldman and any attempts against Shippy or other Chicagoans, she immediately became a prime suspect in the attempt on Shippy's life and found herself forced to hide out in the city she had planned to use as a rallying base.

Alongside the various individual activists, there were a number of thriving liberal publications in the city. It is impossible to determine the exact circulations of newspapers like the *Daily Socialist* and the *Jewish Daily Forward,* or magazines like *The Public*, but they carried significant influence. The *Tribune* and other mainstream newspapers regularly reported on the contents of such magazines, occasionally turning a *Forward* statement on the Averbuch case into front-page news; and figures like Post and Leon Zolotkoff, of the *Daily Courier,* a Yiddish newspaper, used such journalistic positions as springboards to public office.

It took a few days after Averbuch's killing for such periodicals to gather themselves for responses; and when they did, they quickly questioned Shippy's and Sheuttler's approaches to the incident. The *Chicago Daily Socialist* was among the first publications to question Shippy's account of the killing. Determining from the discovery of tefillin in Averbuch's apartment that he had been an orthodox Jew, the paper wrote in a March 3 editorial:

> That the man who was killed was an anarchist has but little proof beyond the fact that anarchist literature was found in his house. He was an extremely orthodox Jew, and that raises a powerful presumption that he was not an anarchist.

The following day, it took to criticizing Scheuttler's handling of the investigation. Under a headline reading "Letters of Shippy's Victim, Translated, Show No Anarchy; Details of Official 'Bunk,'" it wrote:

> While identification of all the letters found in the rooms occupied by Lazarus Averbuch, shot while engaged in a struggle with Chief of Police George M. Shippy, show not one anarchist communication, the police are still making wholesale arrests and lurid accounts of the proposed extermination of all radical societies that are flooding the daily papers.
>
> The arrest of William H. Abramovitz, a student in the night classes at the University of Chicago, was used by the papers to support a story that the university was teeming with anarchy. When this view was expressed to Dr. Charles R. Henderson, noted sociologist and chaplain of the university, he scoffed at it, asserting that very many of the students were Socialists, while none were anarchists. Professor Samuel Harper, son of the late president of the university, gave the same answer.

On the following day, the paper stepped up its attacks against Scheuttler and an investigation it saw as cynically hypocritical:

> Three days of wild newspaper hysteria, three days of police terrorism, three days of wholesale arrests—and at the end Assistant Chief of Police Herman Schuettler has confirmed his first impression that Lazarus Averbuch acted alone when he went to the Shippy home, 21 Lincoln Place at 9 o'clock Monday morning.
>
> Rosa Stern, heralded as the sweetheart of Lazarus Averbuch and said to know the secrets of "a world-wide plot," was found yesterday afternoon hard at work in the tailoring shop of Joseph Biefeld, 230 West Adams

Street, in the Ghetto. She was taken to Schuettler's office in the city hall and subjected to a bitter ordeal of cross questioning by the assistant chief and other members of the police department.

She knew nothing of any plot. She was not even a sweetheart of Lazarus Averbuch. After having three days to think of his body lying in the morgue, subject to all sorts of indignities, she showed no sign which would indicate that Averbuch meant anything to her more than a casual friend.

New York's *Jewish Daily Forward*, a Yiddish newspaper, enjoyed an apparently wide circulation in Chicago, particularly among Jewish socialists. It depended on correspondents in Chicago for its information of the Averbuch incident, but it did not permit distance to prevent it from taking a strong stand against the official story of the event. In an editorial published March 3, it wrote:

What was the story there in Chicago with the shooting in the house of the chief of police?

For the time being it is a deep mystery and it's very likely that it will never be explained. For the only one to have been there from the start, besides the chief of police, was the man who was shot, and he is dead. One is left only with what the chief says, and he himself says nothing that gives even the slightest basis for his claim that the man who was shot was an anarchist and had come to shoot him. All he says is that he had wanted to hand him a letter, but since he "looked like an anarchist" to him, and because he'd dreamt that an anarchist would come and [try to] shoot him, he, the chief, grabbed the stranger around with his hands and called his family to search for weapons in his pockets.

Only one thing is certain right off: it was the stranger who was murdered and the police chief is alive.

But that doesn't prevent all the papers and the police from assuming for certain, as if they had been there, that it was an anarchist who had come to shoot the chief. And that, first thing, will strengthen the incitement against the labor movement and against the movement of the jobless in the whole country. . . . He "looked like an anarchist" to him! As if an anarchist looks different from other people! He looked like an anarchist to him and he dreamed that an anarchist would come and shoot him, that's why he didn't ask for a rabbinic opinion [i.e., didn't go into details] and killed the stranger! Right off, that much is clear.

And the tumult is about "anarchistic crimes"! [i.e., not the crimes of the police chief.]

A mere verdict is unimaginable, until further reports are forthcoming.

The most thoughtful criticism of Shippy's and Schuettler's reactions came from *The Public*, a weekly magazine. In the first issue published after Averbuch's death, publisher Louis Post devoted his lead editorial to the incident. Accepting for the moment the popular suggestion that Averbuch had a "distorted imagination," Post wrote:

The cause of the dead boy's affliction may be reasonably guessed from the fact that he was a Jewish refugee from Kichineff [*sic*], where he had experienced the terrible massacre of his people by a Christian mob under the protection of the Russian police. The particular direction of his homicidal impulse might be fairly attributed to excitement aroused by recent police interference with the peaceable assemblage of the unemployed about whose misfortune he appears to have been deeply concerned; and this morbid feeling may well have been further excited by the announced

intention of the police to suppress an advertised lecture
in which he is reported to have been interested. Such
assertions of police authority, of the lawlessness of
which this alien youth was presumably ignorant, might
not unlikely have identified in his distorted imagination the police system of Chicago with that of Russia,
and given him his insane impulse to assassinate the
chief. At any rate, the boy's homicidal impulse, assuming it to have existed, may be traced with greater reason
along this line of causation than to any "anarchistic"
speeches he may have heard, or "anarchistic" literature
he may have read . . . .

The taking of human life under any circumstance
is a terrible thing. To be sadly deplored even when
necessary, as in self-defense, it is to be sternly condemned if wanton. But there is a species of assassination which by American standards is infinitely worse
than the taking of human life. This is the assassination
of civil liberty. It is worse than the taking of human life
because it involves the taking of human life and more.
To shackle speech and press is to invite destruction. It
always has been so; it always will be so. Yet officials
charged by our laws with protecting free speech and
free press, are proposing to disperse peaceable meetings
and to suppress newspapers for defending unpopular
opinions or opinions that have been branded with
unpopular epithets. Not necessarily from any tender-
ness for particular papers or speakers or agitators or
doctrines or opinions, is it that we should insist upon
free speech and a free press, but for the common good.
Let this anti-American policy of suppression but gain a
foothold against the least popular of meetings and
publications, and no prophet can foresee the lengths to
which it will go. No man of American traditions and
spirit can silently tolerate any reaction, be the pretense
what it may, in the direction of a licensed platform and
a censored press.

Within the first five days after Averbuch's killing, then, the left wing managed to develop a gradual consensus among its disparate members that the investigation precipitated by the killing was a danger in itself. With little political power to take any meaningful action, they did what they could to demonstrate the inconsistency and, indeed, hypocrisy of attacking anarchy by bending or violating the laws of the land.

What they were yet to accomplish in those first few days, however, was to put a dent in the official story as Shippy had first reported it. Although they succeeded in gathering many of the chief's inconsistencies, no one was yet able to present a case suggesting that Averbuch had not been bent on killing the chief. Whether he had been the product of a "distorted imagination" or was the homicidal anarchist Shippy claimed, did not, finally, concern much of the left wing. The chief concern was, understandably, the attack on freedom that Schuettler's zealous investigation represented. It would require more time before anyone thought to question the firmament of the official story: to suggest that Lazarus Averbuch might have been an accidental victim rather than someone killed through the culmination of this own psychotic or social fury.

V

No Room for
Neutrality

The Jewish Community Reacts
March 3–16

If Chicago's left-wing community was drawn immediately into the Averbuch Affair by Shippy's direct attack on it, Chicago's Jewish community entered the fray more slowly. Shippy's original story and the newspapers' handling of it had initially framed the incident as an exclusively anarchist affair. Averbuch, it soon turned out, was a Jew, but Shippy had seen to it that the first reactions against the killing were political, not ethnic.

Nevertheless, Jewish leaders must have known it was only a matter of time before reactions against the killing turned against the Jewish immigrant community from which the alleged assassin had sprung. Many members of the Jewish community, already nervous in an era that saw regular Russian pogroms abroad, found themselves forced to explain how one of their own could participate in so violent and so un-American an attack on American law. They saw that Averbuch's Jewishness could quite easily be held against the entire Jewish community. So, all too aware of how vulnerable the community was, they were forced to anticipate a wave of anti-Semitism.[31]

That the Jews of Chicago considered themselves a single community at all, however, was extraordinary. Jews were divided
among themselves by economic and political differences, time of
immigration, country of origin, and political lines. Many of the
early, established German Jews lived in the prestigious South Side
of Chicago, away from the ghetto area where the newly arrived
immigrants settled.

The first Jews arrived in Chicago in 1840, and by 1880 there
were already 10,000 Jews in the city. The biggest growth, however, took place after 1900. According to estimates made by
one scholar of Chicago Jewish history, the Jewish population
of Chicago grew from 70,000 at the turn of the century to 225,000
by 1920.[32]

The bulk of Chicago's Jewish immigrants before 1880 came
from Germany and parts of the Austro-Hungarian Empire. They
were, in general, well educated and readily absorbed into an ex-
panding mercantile economy. They prospered as the city underwent one of the greatest urban growth spurts ever recorded. The
wealthiest among them stood on equal economic and political
footing—if not equal social ground—with non-Jewish gentry.
Active in charity and public work beyond their numbers, Jewish
immigrants played an important role in humanizing the city for
later, less fortunate arrivals.[33]

Most of the Jews arriving later came from Eastern European
countries, including Poland, the Baltic states, and especially Russia. Anti-Semitism had generally been stronger in those countries than in others in the region. In addition, the immigrants
came mainly from the insular worlds of the ghettos and shtetls.
As a rule they were orthodox in their Jewish observances and
unfamiliar with the customs and conventions of modern Western urban existence. They were the ones who carried their Old
World traditions into Chicago and built up the Jewish ghetto of

the West Side that included, among other things, the European-like Maxwell Street Market.[34]

On the surface, Chicago's established German-speaking Jews seemed to have little in common with the recently arrived East Europeans. People like Adolph Kraus, a leading Jewish lawyer from Bohemia and national president of B'nai B'rith, the largest Jewish fraternal organization in America at that time, and Judge Julian Mack, a prominent Zionist and a close associate of later Supreme Court Justice Louis Brandeis, gave Chicago Jews impressive political champions. In the business area, Julius Rosenwald, chairman of the board of the fast growing Sears, Roebuck corporation and one of the country's wealthiest men, exemplified the achievements of the German Jewish settlers in Chicago. One of their spiritual leaders was Rabbi Emil G. Hirsch, the renowned humanist and leader of Sinai Congregation, a leading congregation of the Reform movement in America.

Yet, for the most part, such figures retained at least a charity relation to their impoverished cousins. Bertha Powell and Mrs. Jacob Schloss oversaw the Miriam Club, where Olga Averbuch lived her first year and a half in the United States. Lazarus Averbuch's English education was enhanced by his studies at the Jewish Training School, which was founded by German Jews and whose Jewish principal was Gabriel Bamberger. Many other prosperous Jews organized relief funds, social services through synagogues, and educational programs for penniless Jews.

Nevertheless, relations between the two different groups were limited. Rather than working to reform the social and economic conditions that made it so difficult for immigrants to find safe, well-paying jobs and to live in sanitary conditions, the Jewish gentry focused their efforts on relief work that, some critics maintained, perpetuated the system that created the hardships they hoped to alleviate. Some wealthy, established Jewish industrialists soon came into conflict with the poor immigrants, who became their source of cheap labor.

When wealthy Jews did participate in programs that questioned the social or economic assumptions of Chicago or America's economy, they generally did so with a low profile. Much of the funding for Jane Addams's Hull House, for instance, came from such Jews, particularly Julius Rosenwald. Because settlement houses were frequently cast as radical, almost revolutionary centers for giving socialists, anarchists, and unionists opportunities to speak publicly, many donors requested anonymity. The Jews who did embrace progressive platforms often found themselves at odds with the Jewish establishment.[35]

Such antagonism was often not limited to the traditional German–East European rivalry. It also existed between established Jews from East European countries themselves. One example of such a dispute was the rivalry between Leon Zolotkoff and Peter Boyarsky. Zolotkoff was a leading Jewish journalist who wrote plays and stories in Hebrew and Yiddish. Born in Vilnius, Lithuania, he came to Chicago in 1887 and helped found the *Jewish Courier*, a Yiddish newspaper. By 1908, he also had become a lawyer, working as an assistant district attorney. A prominent Zionist who went to the First Zionist Congress held in Basel, Switzerland, in 1897, he had risen through the system and, in general, seemed to believe in it. As an editor of the *Jewish Courier*, he was one of the voices of the mainstream Jewish community. Philip P. Bregstone, a later editor of the *Courier* and a critic of Zolotkoff, in recounting the Averbuch Affair, wrote: "I shall omit the part that was played by some of the Jewish politicians who held jobs under the Busse administration; to whom the little jobs they held were more important than the reputation and honor of all the Jews in the United States."[36] Bregstone must have had Zolotkoff in mind, since he was one of the few Jews who held public office in the administration of Mayor Busse.

Boyarsky, a Yiddish writer, humorist, and satirist as well as another of the editors of the *Jewish Courier*, was born in Grodno, Lithuania, in 1866 and came to Chicago at the turn of the century. Outspoken and often unpopular, he fancied himself a voice of the voiceless. Unlike Zolotkoff, he was a gadfly, espousing unpopular causes and often attacking the establishment. In any case, Zolotkoff's name appeared infrequently in defense of Averbuch, while Boyarsky came to play a leading role in the Averbuch case through his articles in the *Courier*.

Both Boyarsky and Zolotkoff worked for Philip Ginsburg, the publisher and managing editor of the *Courier*, traditionally considered a conservative force in the orthodox Jewish community.[37]

When Averbuch was killed, the mainstream Jewish community stood stunned. With few exceptions, its leaders kept quiet or groped for some way to explain how one of their own could have committed such a heinous crime. The *Morning Journal*, a Yiddish daily out of New York, issued an editorial on March 4 that did what it could to reconcile the facts of the case. Beneath a subhead saying, "The wild behavior of a Jewish anarchist is a disgrace and a source of pain for all Jews. The Russian government is the only one that will derive pleasure from [the affair]," it wrote:

> We can only regret the fate of the confused young Jew who paid with his life for the mad attack upon Chicago's Chief of Police, because he simply hadn't understood the situation in which he found himself. A "green" young man can always easily be provoked and when he falls in among those who make it their business to present everything in the darkest colors, one can get him enraged enough to commit the wildest act. The bombastic phrases of the irresponsible agitator

are like oil for the flames of his personal unhappiness. Fantasizing about the "battle" in Russia, he permits himself to be convinced that it is a thousand times worse here. He is much too excited to consider that those who have been here a long time, those who were born here and whose parents were born here don't need to wait for a green Jew to come and "free them from tyrants." Those who mislead, who live from upsetting Jewish parts [of town], make sure that he should not recognize that Americans have totally newer methods for making changes or to bring down officials who don't please them. In the hands of experienced and shrewd agitators, he is like a silly, irresponsible child. The moral responsibility for such an act lies on them, not on him. The blood of Lazarus Averbuch falls on their heads. The shame and the troubles that his wild behavior will naturally result in are their work.

In other words, Averbuch may have done it, but someone else told him to. Because he wasn't yet a real American, it wasn't his fault but rather the fault of mysterious agitators. Since those agitators weren't Jewish, the Jews weren't at fault. Don't rock the boat and the American system will work everything out justly in the end.

That same need to exonerate the Jews as a whole from an act foreign to the faith ran through an editorial voicing the first reaction to the killing in an editorial published in the *Jewish Courier* on March 4. Here, though, the instigation for the killing came not from evil men but from a kind of insanity induced by Russian cruelty. The *Tribune* considered the *Courier*'s statement significant enough to warrant translating and reprinting it for the entire English-speaking community. Under the headline "Organ of the Race in Chicago Laments the Mad Act of Russian Youth," the Tribune reported:

The *Jewish Courier* of yesterday under the caption
'From Kishineff to Chicago' prints the following:

Up to the moment when the *Jewish Courier* went to
press yesterday we hoped that investigation would
reveal that the would-be assassin of Chief of Police
Shippy was not a Jew. We could not possibly believe
that there can be among Jewish radicals a man degenerate and foolish enough to believe that he can better
the world by killing a policeman. We hoped that wise
Providence will have spared the Jews of Chicago and of
the United States the pain and humiliation which such
an act is bound to bring upon any people. Unfortunately our hopes have diminished us. The would-be
assassin of Chief Shippy is a Russian Jew. His name is
Jeremiah Averbuch [*sic*]. His action can mostly be
explained by the fact that he arises from Kishineff and
has witnessed and lived through the Kishineff attacks
upon Jews in which his father was slain and his sisters
ruined [*sic*]. This alone can explain the mental condi-
tion in which this unfortunate would-be murderer was
at the time he planned this act.

For this degenerate and crossed state of his mind,
which was ready to commit murder without reason or
calculation, Jews are not responsible. It is the black
hundreds of Russia who put him in that frame of
mind. They, and they alone, ruined the mind and the
soul of the youthful Averbuch. He was a child of
respectable and well to do Jewish parents. He received a
good education and had a good chance to become a
useful man were it not for the black hundreds.

If he was in any way inclined to melancholy or to
any other mental disorder by heredity, no one ever
noticed it before. The sight of the terrible butcheries of
Jews in Kishineff and in other cities of Russia, the
excitement of the Russian Revolution, the restlessness
and insecurity which marks the life of every Jew in that

acquired country, together with a two years' aimless wandering from place to place and from land to land, have evidently hopelessly unsettled the mind of this unfortunate. In blind frenzy against oppressors and under the impression of the terrorist exploits which are carried out in Russia, his unsettled mind conceived of a plan to kill the Superintendent of Police. In Russia such actions have almost become a fashion at the present time and the unsettled mind of the assassin evidently attempted to carry out a Russian heroic deed upon American soil, and in so doing he has found his own death which he evidently sought.

For the unfortunate Averbuch it is perhaps best that he is dead. With an unsettled mind, his life and surroundings would only be a burden to him. But for the Jews of Chicago and America, he has left a bad legacy. Willingly or unwillingly, every Jew feels some responsibility for Averbuch's shameful deed. Like every other deed of violence, it is bound to hurt the innocent, which is most unfortunate.

Reactions within synagogues seem to have fallen along the same general lines. On March 4, the *Tribune* reported that Rabbi Abraham Hirschberg, of the North Chicago Hebrew Congregation, the first synagogue on Chicago's North Side consisting chiefly of German Jews, characterized Averbuch as a misled youth. He went on to stress that Judaism teaches respect for the laws of nations and was therefore an unlikely breeding ground for bloodthirsty anarchists. The Rabbi seems to have broken new ground, however, in his deploring the fact that Averbuch's religion was so prominently discussed in the reports about the affair. He pointed out that nothing was said of the religion of the assassin of Father Leo Heinrichs in Denver only the month before.

One striking similarity between such attempts to clear the Jewish community of any taint of Averbuch's "crime" is that each treated him coldly and distantly, as either the tool of evil doers or a mind detached from reality. Much like the anarchists who spoke out against the Busse-Scheuttler crackdown, such early defenses of Averbuch were really self-defenses. The way Jews spoke publicly of Averbuch was not the same way they seemed to feel about him privately.

The first significant consideration Jews mustered for Averbuch as a human being came in the sympathy and support they showed Olga Averbuch. Submitted to "sweatbox" methods of interrogation by Shippy and Schuettler, Olga was held in prison for three days. With few friends in the new world, she had literally no one to turn to for help until Bertha Powell and Mrs. Jacob Schloss, her old benefactors from the Miriam Club, came to her defense. Vouching for her character in glowing terms, they probably saved her from further mistreatment and certainly succeeded in obtaining her release more rapidly than otherwise. Perhaps of greatest significance, they also brought her case to the attention of Jane Addams.

While professing to distance themselves from Averbuch himself, some mainstream Jews did attempt to understand who the unfortunate young man had been. As the police investigation failed to turn up any evidence that Averbuch had been active in anarchist circles or even that he had had anything more than a superficial interest in the subject, and as Olga Averbuch continued her vehement insistence that her brother was innocent, various Jews came together to investigate the matter. Bernard Horwich, a noted Chicago philanthropist and Zionist, claimed later to have founded a committee of five to study the affair. Other wealthy Jews began letting it be known quietly that they were willing to donate money so that the truth of the affair might be known.[38]

Such sympathies continued to build as it became clearer and clearer that Shippy's story of what had happened had at least a few obvious inconsistencies. While many left-wing publications announced their skepticism of the official story early, Jews withheld their criticism for a time. The urgent task at hand was to clear the Jewish community from the taint of anarchy; Lazarus Averbuch was simply someone they wished had never arrived in Chicago at all.

That approach to the affair changed suddenly with the publication of an article by Peter Boyarsky. In the *Courier* on March 9, under the heading "Wanted: An American Zola," Boyarsky wrote the first article that tried to clear Averbuch as an individual. Arguing that the "green" young man had been framed by city officials as an attack on Jews citywide, he compared the incident to the Dreyfus Affair of the 1890s. Here was a case of governmental anti-Semitism, he argued, and it would require the talents of an American Emile Zola to clear the unjustly condemned man. Boyarsky may well have thought himself that American Zola, rallying the forces of righteousness to his call.

Reference to Boyarsky's editorial appeared in many of Chicago's newspapers and provoked further editorials by their editors. The charges brought by Boyarsky against Shippy suddenly made the police chief a murderer rather than a helpless victim.

In any event, Boyarsky's article marked a significant shift in the way the affair could be discussed. Only a couple of days before he wrote his piece, the *Courier* had been claiming Jews shouldn't be blamed for the actions of a deranged individual. In that same publication, Boyarsky stopped trying to apologize for the part a Jew played in the story Shippy had told and began to question the basic truths of that story. He was the first thorough skeptic of Shippy's story. He would not be the last.

VI

THE FIGHT FOR CONTROL OF THE STORY

March 5–9

W hat the police had begun as a crackdown on anarchists threatened suddenly to boomerang on them. The recent publications in the press made it possible to attack any and all aspects of the story Shippy had originally told. That story was no longer the universal account of the event that police supporters or critics had either to accept or scorn. The real story, the story of what happened when Lazarus Averbuch left Washburne Avenue and arrived at George Shippy's Lincoln Place address, was suddenly up for grabs.

The police maintained the essence of Shippy's story, of course. No politician as savvy as Mayor Fred Busse and no police officer as canny as Herman Schuettler would repudiate such a close associate, but the administration and police force began making it clear they wanted the episode behind them. As far as they were concerned, Shippy had killed Averbuch in self-defense, and he was entirely innocent. Any questions that might remain unanswered about Averbuch's political affiliation, his motives, or his intent were insignificant. They had a city to keep running.

POLICE TO GREET
RED QUEEN TODAY.

Emma Goldman Now Due in City, and Schuettler Prepares Official Reception.

CENSOR WILL WATCH HER

Open Meeting Addresses Forbidden, and Federal Authorities Plan Deportation.

REDS' PRIESTESS
JOKES OVER NEWS

Emma Goldman Ridicules the Idea That Shippy's Assailant Was Anarchist.

AIDED M'KINLEY CRIME

Teachings of Woman Helped to Inspire Assassination of the President in 1901.

Fig. 12. Newspaper accounts of Emma Goldman's visit.

A loose but growing coalition, however, did what it could to keep the affair alive. As Jews, social advocates, and anarchists regrouped, they began more formally to question everything that had happened. Jewish groups stepped up their repudiation of Shippy and Schuettler's claims. Social reformers like Jane Addams began gathering money to support their inquiries. And the anarchists found something that really annoyed the authorities; they found their leader.

The news that Emma Goldman was coming to Chicago had stirred up police concerns even before the Averbuch shooting. After it, "Red" Emma's arrival sent them into a panic. Knowing that Goldman was due to arrive in the city on either March 4 or 5, the police and city administration tried a two-pronged approach to stopping her. First, they turned to the law and announced it would be illegal for her to speak publicly. Second, they set out to arrest her.

They accomplished their first goal with ease. In a meeting among various city attorneys and Schuettler, they determined to use what the *Inter Ocean* called "plenary use of the present laws to curb anarchy by prohibiting any open meeting at which anarchists might speak, under the broad provisions of the state law which permits the dispersing of any 'unlawful assemblage.'" In a statement issued by Corporation Counsel Brundage, they made clear that such a use of existing law was directly aimed at Emma Goldman:

> A big difficulty of the present condition is the fact that most of these meetings are called ostensibly for other purposes. We have to be very careful not to run counter to the plans of well intentioned persons who want to hold meetings for legitimate purposes. In the case of Emma Goldman, we know that whenever she talks, she talks anarchy and so there will be no difficulty in forbidding her to speak.

Moreover, the police seem to have resolved at the same meeting, or at essentially the same time, to condemn any site that dared to permit Goldman to speak.

The second part of the police strategy went much less smoothly. Intending to arrest Goldman for questioning about the Averbuch affair, Schuettler and his men simply couldn't find her. Despite searching the homes of friends she had stayed with during her last visit to the city and keeping a close watch on anarchist haunts, they were always a half hour too late or a couple of doors away from catching her. Goldman, of course, made great fun of the police for their failures. In an interview on March 6 with a reporter from the *Chicago American* who had managed to track her down, she said:

> If the police want me, of course they will arrest me. But I can't see what charges they can make against me. I intend to speak and insist on the right of free speech. If the police stop me, then it is up to them to explain why. My subject will be "Anarchism as It Really Is." I expect to be in Chicago two weeks and will deliver a number of lectures. It amuses me to hear that the police are looking for me and can't find me. I have no intention to conceal myself. I would go down to City Hall this minute if I had any business there, but, of course, I shall not go out of my way to go there.

In an exchange of newspaper sallies, Schuettler responded in kind. Hearing that Goldman had vowed she would find an audience for her lecture, he said to the *Inter Ocean* on March 7, "If that is all that is worrying Emma, I am willing to give her an audience of patrolmen in some squadroom some time. But she will not be allowed to speak at any public meeting and that settles it." The truth remained, however, that he and his men were still unable to find her. They were able to prevent her from speaking or making much of an impression on the city—although rumors of her whereabouts and intentions were front-page news in most papers that week—but could not entirely stifle her. Nothing, insofar as Emma Goldman was concerned, was settled.

While the doings of Goldman and her game of mouse-and-cat with the police stole most of the headlines, a number of developments took place in the Averbuch case itself. On March 5, Schuettler announced that he had abandoned his earlier theory that Averbuch had been part of a conspiracy to kill Shippy. Announcing he was convinced Averbuch had acted alone, he continued:

> I am going ahead, however, arresting all his friends I can find in the effort to sift this tragedy to the bottom . . .
>
> Every clue that was furnished by Olga Averbuch, the would-be assassin's sister; Harry Goldstein, secretary of the Edelstadt group of anarchists; Isadore Maron, Averbuch's friend; M. Abromovitz, the student; and Miss Stern was followed without revealing a shred of evidence . . . .

Convinced he already had his man—in the city morgue—Schuettler would soon begin calling for the case to be closed altogether.

Meanwhile, Jane Addams had convened a group of social activists and concerned Jews who weren't sure they wanted the case to be closed yet. The core of Addams's theory of social service was that strangers generally disliked one another because they were unfamiliar with one another's habits and customs. As a result, she worked throughout her life to get to know different peoples in different cultures in order to mediate their problems and concerns to the community at large. For the Averbuch Affair, she called together Julius Rosenwald; S. S. Gregory, a past president of the American Bar Association; Judge Julian Mack; and Harold Ickes, a recent law school graduate from the University of Chicago who was already a well-established political gadfly.

The first order of business was to raise sufficient funds to investigate the case more fully. Rosenwald reportedly pledged $2,000 immediately, but did so on condition that his name not be brought into the investigation. Other wealthy and not-so-wealthy people contributed as well, but it is not known exactly how much Addams was able to raise. Newspapers regularly reported the Addams group had a fund of $10,000 at its disposal. One report claims the group had as much as $40,000.[39] Whatever the truth, there was at least enough money to pursue the investigation and enough publicity to make police officials uneasy.

The second task of the Addams committee was to find an attorney to represent Olga Averbuch's interests at the coroner's inquest scheduled for March 18—and later postponed to March 24. The job turned out to be more difficult than Addams and the others might have expected. The logical choice would appear to have been Clarence Darrow, the country's leading civil rights lawyer and a native Chicagoan. Darrow, however, was just then recuperating from a severe illness he had developed during a recent court battle in Boise, Idaho, to free Bill Haywood and his codefendants on charges of murdering the governor of Idaho. The *Chicago Tribune* quoted Darrow as saying that he had never been asked by Jane Addams to handle the Averbuch case.

The committee then turned to S. S. Gregory, one of its members and an important behind-the-scenes player in keeping the case alive. Gregory had first gained national exposure as one of the team of attorneys who represented the Haymarket Square leaders. As a respected national figure from his work with the American Bar Association, he would have given immediate credibility to the case. What's more, his experience from the

Haymarket trial would have taught him how to handle the extraordinary pressures such a politically charged trial would likely generate. Gregory refused the offer, however, claiming that he had needed to work nearly a decade to restore his professional standing after the Haymarket Affair, and that, with a wife and family to support, he could not jeopardize his future income by accepting such a commission.

The committee turned then to John Harlan, the Democratic candidate Busse had defeated for mayor in 1905. A noted populist, Harlan was one of the most visible attorneys in the city. The mere rumor that he had agreed to take the case created news. New York's *Daily Forward* on March 15, announcing—incorrectly as it turned out—that Harlan had agreed to the case, called him "Chicago's most prominent attorney." It went on to say, "The fact that Harlan, the son of Justice Harlan of the U.S. Supreme Court and a person of considerable influence, has taken the case shows that a great battle is brewing between the police and the entire Jewish and radical movement in Chicago." Harlan had not agreed to take the case, however; where his sympathies in the affair lay was not clear.

Patrick O'Donnell, another prominent attorney, was also reported to have accepted the case, this time by the *Inter Ocean* on March 11. O'Donnell was best known as the headline cocounsel for the recently acquitted Dora Feldman McDonald, with the flamboyant J. Hamilton Lewis as his cocounsel. In what had been the city's featured show trial just a month before, O'Donnell and Lewis had successfully defended Dora, a Jew and the widow of one of the city's most prominent political bosses, against charges she had murdered a young lover who had threatened to spurn her. The fact that she was Jewish and that he and Lewis had managed to make themselves the focus of much of the trial's reporting would certainly have made O'Donnell an attractive candidate for Addams and the other members of the group. As it was,

O'Donnell did not accept Averbuch's case, and it is not clear the group ever approached him at all.

The group Addams convened saw itself involved in a legal battle. The activities it undertook—the hiring of an attorney and an expert coroner—should not have been newsworthy themselves; but, because so much of the affair was being played out in public, every step, even a behind-the-scenes one, had a sensational side to it. This was so because the newspapers had effectively established themselves as the keepers of the playing field for the story as it developed. It was growing increasingly clear that the final battle to determine what had happened to Lazarus Averbuch would not be determined in a courtroom; it would be won or lost by the ability of one side or the other to tell its story to the city through the medium of its newspapers.

It should not be surprising then that on March 9, exactly a week after the shooting, Averbuch's chief supporters and chief accusers unveiled dramatic new wrinkles in the stories they were telling the public. On that day, the police announced they had discovered the pawnbroker who sold Averbuch the weapons he used in his assassination attempt. Meanwhile, Olga Averbuch had given an extensive and emotional interview to the Yiddish *Jewish Courier*, which in English translation appeared as a letter in most newspapers in the city. It was punch and counterpunch in the fight to tell the story.

Only four days after establishing that Averbuch had worked alone, Schuettler brought forward John Corbly, a pawnbroker with a shop at 110 North Clark Street. It was Corbly, he claimed, who had sold Averbuch the knife, gun, and bullets used in the assassination attempt. Corbly confirmed Schuettler's claim and grew more and more certain of the details of the sale in the days following Schuettler's announcement. On March 14, the *Daily Socialist* quoted him:

> I distinctly remember the sale. I identified the body as that of the man to whom I sold the revolver and the knife shown me by Chief Shippy. The sale was made between 4 and 4:30 o'clock Saturday afternoon—not later than 4:30. There can be no doubt in my mind of these facts. The matter is indelibly stamped on my memory.

Schuettler shared the additional detail that Corbly and Averbuch had haggled over the price of the weapons before settling on four dollars.

If Schuettler's and Corbly's claims were true, then there would be little doubt Averbuch had intended to kill Shippy when he went to his home the following Monday morning. Averbuch's supporters assailed the new story immediately. Olga Averbuch, in her statement to the *Courier*, claimed Lazarus had not had any money to buy such weapons. If he had somehow gotten them anyway, she was certain he had never brought them into their home. What was more, even if Lazarus had somehow obtained and secreted a gun, it would have done him no good since he had never had the opportunity to learn how to shoot.

The *Daily Socialist* questioned the story from the beginning. It sent a reporter to Eichengreen's Egg Company to speak with Eichengreen himself about Averbuch's whereabouts the day Corbly claimed to have sold him the weapons. "[Averbuch] was here until 4:30," Eichengreen told the reporter. "He usually worked until 5:30, but on this Saturday night, work was somewhat slack and work was stopped at 4:30." Averbuch, quite clearly, could not have been to Corbly's pawn shop before 4:30 if he had been at work that late.

More conspiratorial and more potentially damning were intimations that Corbly was somehow in the employ of the police themselves. Several figures concerned with the case, most prominently the assistant state's attorney and the *Daily Courier* editor Zolotkoff, pointed out that Corbly, as a pawnbroker, owed his license and therefore livelihood to the goodwill of the police department. Others suggested that Corbly's testimony may have been "bought" in exchange for his being permitted to continue running his shop despite having a criminal record. As Zolotkoff said in a statement reported by the *Daily Socialist* on March 13, "Who but one dealer in firearms who is under heavy obligation to the police has shown that Averbuch ever had a revolver or dagger. I do not believe that he had either when he entered Chief Shippy's house." Zolotkoff's and others' skepticism of Shippy's original story—skepticism that went so far as to suggest that Averbuch may have been unarmed when he visited Shippy—was testimony to the effect Olga Averbuch's letter, published earlier in the week, was beginning to have.

Of all the people most immediately hurt by the shooting of Averbuch, his sister Olga must surely have suffered the most. Arrested almost immediately by Schuettler and his men, she was subjected to sweatbox tactics of interrogation and held in custody for three or four days without being permitted any contact with friends or supporters. She had not been told of her brother's death, but had been led up to his corpse in what police hoped would be a technique to shock her into a confession. He was her only family in the New World and, alone and virtually friendless, she made a pathetic figure.

When social workers finally obtained her release, she walked from the cloister of her prison cell into a city that buzzed with rumors about her brother. She must surely have been shocked to see he was being depicted as a wild-eyed anarchist assassin. The

Fig. 13. Olga Averbuch.
Photograph: *Chicago Daily News.* Chicago Historical Society. DN–005868.

brother she had known was quite different from the fanatic Chief
Shippy claimed to have shot in self-defense. On March 8, when
she agreed to grant a five-hour interview with Morris Silbert of
the *Daily Courier,* she made her first public comment on the entire affair. Different parts of her statement appeared in different
papers. The original *Courier* papers are lost, but the *Courier* did
print the following account by Olga at length:

My brother, Jeremiah Averbuch, came to this city
three months ago from the town of Czernowitz,
Bukovina, Austria, where my family have lived since
the massacre of Jews in Kishineff. My brother came to
this city with a double purpose—first, to earn a little
money and help our family, and, second, for my sake,
that I might not be so lonesome in the new, free world.
As soon as he came he was very anxious to get work.

When I begged him to take a few weeks' rest, he
replied that he did not come here to rest, but to work,
in order that he might be able to help the people at
home. I got a job for him at which he earned $6 a
week. He paid $3 a week for board, and the rest that
remained, besides his expenses for dress and other
necessities, he sent home. Only last week we sent 10
rubles to Czernowitz, and in order to be able to send
that amount he had to give away the last $3 which he
had. He regretted that he was not able to send more,
and constantly made plans how to get a better position
in order to be able to send more money home and
bring the rest of our family to this country.

A few days before this terrible tragedy, he told me
that he hoped to get a good position on a railroad. He
also made plans to go into the country if his railroad
job should turn out to be a failure.

You ask me what business he had to go to Chief
Shippy. I cannot give an exact answer, because he did
not tell me that he was going there. But I am certain
that his object in going was to ask the chief for a record
or certificate of good behavior, as is customary in
Russia. You know that in Russia every office demands a
certificate of good behavior from the home police
office of every applicant for a position, and especially
from the chief of police. He thought therefore that such
a certificate would help him procure a good position.

One thing I can tell you with certainty. My brother
had no revolver. He never handled a revolver and did

not know how to shoot. If he had a revolver, I would have known of it, and to buy a revolver just before he went to see Chief Shippy he had no money.

My brother was never an anarchist. Your chief of police whom you crowned as a great hero is a plain murderer. He shot my brother without cause or reason. He did it either because he was a coward or a cold-blooded murderer who wanted to win a name for himself as a hero, as the newspapers made him out to be, my friends inform me. I cannot point out the reason why Shippy shot my brother, but I know that my brother never had weapons of any kind.

The papers stated that they found in my rooming place a box with revolver bullets. That is an absolute lie. He had no bullets because he did not need them. He had no gun and did not know how to use one. If a revolver and knife were placed beside my brother's dead body, it was done in Chief Shippy's house, and as he was dead he could not deny.

How old was my brother? He would have been 19 at the next Passover holidays, about five weeks hence.

Do you believe he went to the chief's house to shoot him? If he really wanted to shoot the chief, and if he really had a revolver, why could not he shoot him when the chief stepped into his carriage? Why could not he shoot him while handing him the letter? My brother was neither a fool nor insane. He went to seek bread, and he met his death where he expected it least. He was shot without cause, without reason, and the knife, revolver, bullets and all kinds of papers were put beside him afterward.

Do you believe that Chief Shippy could not overpower a boy of 19 in his, the Chief's, own house? Why, there were seven persons against one. Chief Shippy, this Goliath, who, as I am told, is more than six foot tall and weighs more than 200 pounds, this veteran policeman, could have ground my brother into

the dust by only taking him in his hands. Is it possible
that the chief, his son, his coachman, his wife, his
niece, and his daughter could not bind my brother and
arrest him if Shippy were not eager for blood, if he
were not eager to murder? Would it not have been
sufficient for him to wound him? Why was it necessary
to shoot into him seven bullets? Why did he keep on
shooting when he already lay wounded on the floor in
the dark hall? Does this not prove that Chief Shippy
shamelessly murdered him? Does this not show that
my brother's blood was shed innocently? Is not Chief
Shippy the Cain who murdered his weaker brother?
Will the blood of my brother be silenced in his grave?

My brother left his home Monday morning, a
couple of hours before he was murdered. In my
statement to the police I made a mistake. I said that he
did not stay at home Sunday night. I said this because I
became frightened and excited when detectives
swooped down upon me Monday evening and suddenly showed me a picture of my brother, saying that
he had murdered three men and was himself killed. I
had just finished my supper, after having waited a long
while for him to come. Then I left a note for my
brother that I went out to take a walk and he should
not worry at not finding me home.

At that moment I heard the tramping of feet in the
hallway. I listened and was startled because I had never
heard such rough steps in my hall before. It never
happened that several people should come all at once
to my house at night. I opened the door and a crowd of
detectives and reporters entered my room. Does
Averbuch live here? I was asked. And when I said yes
they showed me a picture of my brother and told me
he had killed three persons.

You can imagine how I felt at that moment. I
expected my brother to come home well, and instead

such news was brought me. It seemed to me as if ages had passed since I had seen him. My thoughts became confused and I made the mistake of saying that he had not been home Sunday. He spent last Sunday at the theater and Sunday evening he was home, reading in the company of friends.

Detectives searched me from head to foot. They searched every nook and corner of the house. One detective found a small bottle which contained castor oil and he took it for a chemical used in the making of bombs. He gave it to the other detectives. They smelled it, examined it and expressed their opinion that it was some dangerous substance which anarchists used in the making of bombs.

They hurried me to the station and there they bombarded me with different questions. I had to stand it all, of course. But I could not say what I did not know. They sent to me my brother's employer, Mr. Eichengreen, hoping that he would find out from me whether my brother was connected with an anarchistic plot. Mr. Eichengreen was always very kind to me. He begged me to confess everything. But what could I confess when I knew of no plots and knew that my brother did not belong to any anarchistic organizations?

I know that they killed my brother without reason. Besides Mr. Eichengreen, they sent to me an elderly woman who begged me that I should make her happy by telling "all about the conspiracy." This woman at once handed me a dollar. I refused her money and told her what I thought.

You came to me for a statement in the name of the *Jewish Courier*. I told you everything, and for this I beg and demand that the *Courier* should try and do me the favor to see, first, that my brother should be buried according to the Jewish law, and, second, I beg you to

print my statement just as I give it to you in order that
the entire population of Chicago may hear the appeal
of a wounded and broken heart. Perhaps this will bring
justice.

Although the *Tribune* and some other mainstream papers
printed considerably smaller portions of the statement as a letter—and eliminated the most sensational parts altogether—the
gist of her message was indeed spread to the entire population of
Chicago. It would not be easy to ignore the appeal of Olga's
"wounded and broken heart."

In fact, Olga's statement played so skillfully on the emotional
aspects of the case and wove so much of the defense's case in and
out of her own fears that many people immediately suspected
Olga herself either had a great deal of assistance in putting the
statement together or had almost nothing to do with it at all. Just
as acknowledging the story of Corbly the pawnbroker would have
conceded Averbuch's murderous intent, so would recognizing
Olga's claim to having been consistently mistreated concede the
need for a further investigation into the affair.

The most vocal skeptics were, of course, the police. Shippy
himself told the *Tribune* on March 9:

> I do not think any attention should be paid to this
> letter supposed to have been written by the Averbuch
> girl. The source of the knife and gun Averbuch had has
> been established beyond question. While the police are
> doing all in their power to quell the spirit of anarchy, I
> do not think it is right that so much publicity should
> be given the anarchist leaders and their doings. Let the
> matter die down and the police will take care of the
> situation.

Schuettler used stronger language to say nearly the identical things. In an interview with the *Inter Ocean* also on March 9 he said:

> It is perfectly ridiculous to think of paying attention to that letter of Olga Averbuch. I think she had little to do with the writing of it. It has been positively established that Averbuch bought the knife and gun at the Clark Street shop that Saturday before the shooting took place and gave his address when he made the purchase. The occasion does not demand that Chief Shippy be defended. There will be no investigation, that is for certain.

No investigation meant no further investigation. With Corbly's story now a part of the official police story of what took place, Schuettler had introduced what he expected to be the final piece of the Averbuch puzzle.

Barely a week and a half into the mystery of the shooting, the story was less clear than it had ever been. The police and other critics had raised questions about the authorship of Olga Averbuch's statement at the same time that Averbuch's supporters cast doubt on the story Corbly told. At the center of all the uncertainty, however, was the question of who Lazarus Averbuch was. If Shippy and Schuettler were right and he had been a devious and sinister anarchist, then he might well have developed and attempted to carry out an involved assassination plot. Yet Olga Averbuch, the person who knew him better than anyone else in the New World, claimed he could not have been the person the police made him out to be. He was naive and innocent, she claimed; but, considering the stakes behind the claim, it was hard to know just how much of her story to believe.

VII

THE FIGHT CONTINUES

TUG-OF-WAR OVER AVERBUCH'S BODY

March 9–16

The nub of the mystery still remained. Who was Lazarus Averbuch? Even in death he was finding Chicago a world that could not make a place for him. Subjected to the most contradictory claims, his character was disputed in headlines in the same newspapers that just days before had displayed photos of his dead and puffy face. Not able to rest comfortably in death, he would still have a role to play in the affair of his own killing, a remarkably ghoulish role.

Despite Schuettler's avowal to the contrary, Averbuch's supporters in the Jewish and progressive communities were determined to see that the circumstances of his death were investigated. The group that Jane Addams assembled was already working to honor Olga's first request, that the investigation be a thorough one, but it was her second request—that her brother receive a proper Jewish burial—that suddenly took center stage. The next week would see headlines all across the city chronicling the efforts of Averbuch's supporters to find a final resting place for him.

Stymied in their efforts to find an attorney who would agree to take the case, the Addams group turned its efforts to finding an expert pathologist who would agree to conduct a second autopsy on Averbuch's body. With the gradual eroding of Shippy's credibility, it seemed possible that a more careful examination of the corpse would show some wrinkles that the initial autopsy—made by Busse-appointee coroner Peter Hoffman—had overlooked or, perhaps, left unreported.

In this search, the group seems to have had no difficulty at all in retaining its first choice, Dr. Ludwig Hekteon, a faculty member at Rush Medical College. Calling him a "famous pathologist," the *Tribune* went on to report on March 13 that he had "been retained by the same influential interests that secured Mr. Harlan as legal representative." John Harlan had not, as it turned out, been retained, but the comparison demonstrated how eminent Hekteon was. The investigation, despite Schuettler's hopes, was moving forward.

With Hekteon officially hired, the pressure on the Addams group to find an attorney redoubled. They needed to have someone present during the second autopsy in order to make use of any of Hekteon's findings at the upcoming coroner's inquest. Rebuffed in their efforts to hire a "name" attorney, they turned at last to someone in their midst. Harold Ickes, a recent law school graduate, had been advising Olga Averbuch and Jane Addams from the start, and now, by default, would have to become the leader of the defense. As he wrote of it later, "[Addams] said, 'Well Mr. Ickes, it looks as if you would have to do it. Will you?' "[40]

There was no mistaking why Ickes chose to take a case that could so easily have hurt his professional prospects even as his legal career was just beginning. He did it because he believed in fighting a system that allowed men like Fred Busse to prosper. In his *Autobiography of a Curmudgeon*, published in 1943, he spoke scornfully of Busse and his associates. Referring to Charles Yerkes, who had held a monopoly on the transit system in the city, and Samuel Insull, who made a fortune controlling the city's utilities, Ickes wrote, "Yerkes, Busse and Insull helped to sharpen my teeth for Mussolini, Hirohito and Hitler." He continued:

> I still craved Fred Busse's blood, while the *Tribune* still salaamed before him. Not that it [Busse's blood] wouldn't in all probability have poisoned me. Busse had cheated Chicago out of a capable mayor—John Harlan. He had smeared another—Mayor Dunne— and cut short the latter's usefulness in Chicago politics, although in 1912 Dunne was to be elected governor. By means of cunning propaganda, Busse had been foisted on the people, which was bad for them. Everything worthwhile had wilted under his slimy touch, although he was careful to keep up superficial appearances. If the *Tribune* was for him, so was the underworld. So, as sometimes happens, were respectable citizens, includ- ing the deacons, the elders, and many of the preachers. So were the "interests" that did "business"—funny business mostly—with the city. Truly a formidable combination![41]

Ickes had developed a personal relationship with Harlan when he supported the attorney in his unsuccessful bid for mayor in 1904. And so, when Ickes first sought a law office, Harlan gave him permission to work out of his own suite. The erroneous press reports that Harlan had agreed to take the case may well have grown out of some confusion over Ickes's working relationship with Harlan. He was not, as was sometimes reported, Harlan's associate. He merely shared some of Harlan's office space. Ickes wrote later of how much he had admired his early benefactor, but Harlan found the publicity around the Averbuch trial too much even to be in its glow. He soon asked Ickes to find new office space for himself, and he effectively ended their friendship.

After the initial, undeniably shameful treatment of Averbuch's body, it was sent to coroner Peter Hoffman. Hoffman was a political appointee of Fred Busse and someone who entertained ambitions beyond his coroner post. He and his associates had initially performed a hasty inspection on the remains and reported that Averbuch had been struck by five bullets, three of which would have produced fatal wounds. What happened after the autopsy is not entirely clear. On March 6, the *Inter Ocean*, generally one of the more responsible and temperate papers in the city, reported that somehow, someone had "lost" Averbuch's body. Its front-page headline read, "Body of Slain 'Red' Vanishes Going to Tomb—Mysterious Disappearance of Averbuch's Corpse Puzzles Police, Who Investigate Whether Anarchists, Sister or Medical Students Stole It." The article read, in part:

> To mystery surrounding his life and mystery in the motive for his attack on Chief of Police Shippy, another mystery was added last night when the body of Lazarus Averbuch, the Russian Jew assassin, disappeared.
>
> The body was sent from the county morgue to be taken to Dunning [cemetery] at 4:30 o'clock in the afternoon. It was to be buried in the potter's field, but it failed to reach the poor farm . . . .
>
> Where the body is no one can explain.
>
> "I hired an undertaker to take the body away and see to its burial," said Coroner Hoffman.
>
> Later in the evening Dr. Davis, superintendent of the county morgue, said, "The body was taken to the potter's field in the county wagon."

Strangely, none of the other major papers in town carried the story about Averbuch's body; the incident went without mention in the *Tribune* and *Daily News*. The *Daily Socialist* reported the burial in potter's field had gone on without a hitch, citing the exact lot in which the body had been buried.

Other newspaper reports centered rather on what was widely depicted as "bizarre" behavior on Olga Averbuch's part. During a ceremony that most papers reported taking place in potter's field, Olga was said to have been on the brink of hysteria. She would not give her statement to the *Jewish Courier* for two days yet, so she remained a mystery to the public. They read that Olga insisted on having a photograph taken of her with her arm draped around her brother's body, and that she broke down screaming and sobbing across her brother's coffin as it was being lowered into the ground. If Olga had actually been in hysterics, one source of her unhappiness was likely that she had as yet sought in vain to have her brother buried according to Jewish custom. Friends and sympathizers had managed to collect almost a hundred dollars for the burial, but not a single Jewish undertaker or rabbi had come forth to conduct the services. Most seem to have felt Lazarus Averbuch had disgraced the Jewish community; to have agreed to grant him such services would somehow have acknowledged the Jews' collective guilt in his assassination attempt.

Whatever may actually have happened with Averbuch's body or at its burial, there appear to have been irregularities about the whole business. To begin with, Hoffman had shipped the body out in the evening—the same evening that Olga Averbuch and her friend Rosie Stern were first released from jail—against usual procedure. Second, it was raining heavily at the time the body was supposed to have been buried, certainly making the task more difficult. And third, the entire business took place with unusual haste, probably to thwart the assorted socialists and anarchists who might have been interested in staging some kind of rally at the burial. In any event, it turned out that Lazarus Averbuch was not ready for his permanent rest.

In the meantime, Emma Goldman and her fellow anarchists continued their own efforts to force a retelling of Averbuch's killing. She took few pains to elude the police, who continued their search for her, because she, Miriam Yampolsky, William Nathanson, and Lucy Parsons were busy seeking a site that would permit them to stage the lectures she had been promising to give. The search was proving a frustrating one. There was certainly no shortage of lecture halls in Chicago, but Schuettler and other administration officials always seemed to be one step ahead of them. No sooner would they find a venue agreeing to lease its space to them than the police would coerce the landlord into withholding permission.

They were convinced they had at last found a spot, however, when the irascible Ben Reitman contacted them with a promise to supply a vacant store that he had used on occasion as the headquarters for the Brotherhood Welfare Association, the self-help organization he ran with and for hobos. It was a big site, but it was rundown and filthy. As if he were answering someone's prayers, though, Reitman assured them it would be ready. Mustering a crew of hobos, he made good on his promise. By the morning of March 14, the day the lecture was scheduled, the place was a legitimate auditorium.

That afternoon, however, Reitman was visited by officials from the building and fire departments. Although he and the other organizers had set up seats for 250 people, Reitman, sensing the inspectors were out to trap him, told them he was expecting a crowd of only fifty. "Nine," the building official said, meaning no more than nine could be permitted. The fire inspector added,

"The place is not safe for more." At the last moment, the best chance yet for Goldman to find a place to speak had been quashed.[42]

Although the meeting itself came to nought, the planning for it marked the first time Goldman and Reitman met. Goldman claimed later to have been fascinated immediately by the man who would subsequently become her lover, grand distraction, chief promoter, and decade-long traveling companion. Reitman in turn seems to have been attracted to her immediately as well, but to him, the roguish doctor, infatuation was nothing unusual. How much their incipient relationship affected the doings of the Averbuch Affair is unclear, but it did help Goldman in her efforts to avoid the authorities: the last place they'd have sought the doctrinaire revolutionary would have been in the bed of one of the city's most notorious womanizers.

With the hiring of Hekteon and Ickes, Averbuch's supporters were ready to undertake the second autopsy of his body. Although they seem to have had no difficulty finding the body, where it had been remains a mystery. The *Tribune* and *Daily Socialist*, along with most other papers, claimed it had been buried in grave 1,196, block 1, at Dunning Cemetery, in what was known as potter's field, the poor farm. They continued to make no mention of any controversy about the original burial, tacitly denying the story that the *Inter Ocean* held as front-page news.

Even as late as March 13, the day the exhumation took place, the *Inter Ocean* stuck by its original story. Averbuch's body had been "lost," it claimed. Hinting at some conspiracy, it quoted representatives of the Jewish Free Burial Society (the *Gomle Chesed shel Emeth*) in support. "That burial was a fake," declared A. M. Liebling, the society's secretary. He went on:

I went to the Maxwell Street Settlement on Clinton
Street this morning. Olga Averbuch was there. Miss
Field, the head of the settlement, told me that the girl
could see no one, and that her lawyer had advised her
to see no one, and not to sign any burial permits. She
refused to tell me who this "lawyer" was.

The *Jewish Free Press*, the paper of which I am the
editor, comes out tomorrow morning. In this issue we
demand explanation of the treatment given the body of
Lazarus Averbuch. It was not buried on the day announced, nor on the following day, and it never has
been in grave 1,196 at Dunning.

Paul Witkowsky, the society's president, echoed him. Sounding
the most suspicious of a conspiracy, he said:

The Jewish Free Burial Society believes that the article
printed in the *Inter Ocean* several days ago about the
disappearance of the body of Lazarus Averbuch was
absolutely true. Mystery in connection with its disposi-
tion has been increased every day since, and the
authorities, instead of trying to clear up the situation,
have clouded it. Somebody has been trying to hide
something, and we are going to find out who and what.

Neither the society nor the *Inter Ocean* seems ever to have been
able to make its claims widely accepted, but the fact that they
could press them with such vehemence, over such time, and in so
public a forum indicates perhaps more than anything else the
extent to which the credibility of all the parties concerned in the
affair had been damaged. It was getting increasingly difficult to
know what to believe about Lazarus Averbuch and the doings
around him.

The autopsy itself, which was held in what the newspapers
called "the morgue of the insane asylum," took place in great se-

crecy. The only people admitted were Ickes, Hekteon, two assistants, Hoffman, three policemen, and undertaker Lewis Hamburg. It seems to have been the first time Ickes and Hekteon met, and they spoke so little to one another during the examination itself that Hekteon later told the *Tribune,* on March 13, that he had no way of getting in touch with the attorney. "I wanted to call him up tonight," he said, "but I could not recall how he spelled his name and could not locate it in the directory."

Hekteon promised reporters he would issue a report on his findings "in a couple days," but preliminary accounts of the autopsy came out even more quickly. The next day, March 14, Hamburg, who had at last agreed to bury Averbuch, reported to the *Tribune* what he had found most interesting as he observed the autopsy. Whether he knew it or not, he also cast serious doubts on Shippy's original story that Shippy and his driver Foley had both shot Averbuch as he stood between them at the landing of his front stairs. In his statement to the *Tribune*, Hamburg said:

> Two bullet holes particularly attracted my attention. One through the left side, which entered between the fourth and fifth ribs, went out between the ninth and tenth ribs at the back. This shows, as I understand such matters, the shot was from above. The other bullet hole which attracted my attention was made on the right side where a bullet which struck the clavicle had made no abrasion on the flesh. This also caused me to believe Averbuch was shot from above.
>
> One bullet was removed and Sergeant Scribner and another detective started a dispute as to whether it was of thirty-two or thirty-eight caliber. The bullet is now in the hands of the police.

Shippy owned a .32 caliber gun; Foley had, and Averbuch was supposed to have had, a .38. It would not be until the coroner's inquest that the full relevance of Hekteons's findings would become clear. What would not become clear then, however, was the most dramatic moment of this second autopsy, a moment ghoulish enough to suggest that speculation concerning a missing corpse was certainly plausible; this time, his brain was missing. The tale of the "missing brain" is recounted at length in Harold Ickes's private papers, which were unsealed in recent years.[43]

Early in the proceedings of the second autopsy, as Ickes, someone with no training in medicine or pathology, watched, he noticed a heated conference between Hoffman and an attendant. The attendant left the morgue quickly, stirring Ickes's interest. Asking the other trained personnel in the room, he learned Averbuch's brain had not been in the corpse that was unearthed. It seemed that, during the first examination of the body, Hoffman had sent Averbuch's brain out to be examined in greater detail. There were earlier newspaper reports citing experts who claimed that Averbuch's brain had been normal, without any anarchist characteristics. Hoffman had, however, never retrieved the brain afterwards. He had had Averbuch buried without the brain in violation of decency and in violation of Jewish law. According to Ickes, the brain was recovered, but Hoffman was very embarrassed by the matter.[44]

There still remained the task of finally burying Lazarus Averbuch according to Jewish law. On March 13, just hours after the second autopsy was completed, Averbuch was finally buried for good in Ridgelawn, a Jewish cemetery on Chicago's northwest side, in a plot owned by the Jewish Free Burial Society. The ceremony was quiet, with few in attendance.

Although no anarchists or socialists had explicitly stated they intended to turn Averbuch's funeral into a political event, it seemed likely they would. Whether they accepted Averbuch as one of their own or depicted him as the innocent victim of the machinations of government, he was still an effective symbol for them. With Olga Averbuch still shaken and on the verge of a total breakdown, however, such a politicization of the event might genuinely have upset her. With Schuettler further opposed to giving the radicals any opportunity to come together in solidarity, an unlikely alliance was born: the Addams group and the police agreed that the burial should be swift and surreptitious.

The first hurdle they faced together, however, was that no Jewish undertaker would agree yet to handle the case. It meant a great deal to Olga that her brother receive the proper Jewish rites, so the near universal opposition on the part of the undertakers also threatened to precipitate her collapse. At last they managed to contact Hamburg, the undertaker for the first burial, at his office at 3725 Cottage Grove Avenue. Despite pressure from the Jewish Free Burial Society, among others, he agreed to donate his services for the second burial. In a statement he made to the *Tribune* the following day, March 14, he said:

> The first I knew of the intended second burial was early Thursday morning [March 12, the day before the burial and autopsy] when J. Weinberg, an undertaker on Fourteenth Street, near Halsted Street, called me up by telephone and asked me to have nothing to do with the ceremony.
>
> I replied I did not care for advice from other undertakers.
>
> About 11 o'clock I received another telephone message to meet Miss Addams and others interested in the Averbuchs in rooms 1132-4-8 Marquette Building, the offices of John Maynard Harlan. I went and met Miss Addams, Mrs. Raymond Robins, Miss

Breckenridge, Miss Mary Field, Attorney Harold Ickes
and several other persons whom I do not know.
     I was informed of the proposed removal and told
that the utmost secrecy was to be maintained. Simply
out of charity's sake I agreed to remove the body. I
went to the city hall with Miss Field in an automobile
and secured the permit for disinterment.

In his 1939 autobiography, Bernard Horwich, already a
prominent Jewish leader in 1908, wrote that he helped to arrange
the reinterment with "the assistance of men from *The Jewish Courier.*"[45] Horwich gives no further details, though his claim seems
to indicate that mainstream Jewish organizations were involved
in the Averbuch affair, an involvement that was not otherwise
apparent in the public press. In any event, Averbuch at last had
come to a final resting place. His unmarked grave is in a plot of
ground containing the remains of Jews who died penniless.

     The boy from Kishinev who had fled to the United States in
order to build a new life for himself and his family had run afoul
of the American Dream. Yet, buried or not, Averbuch was still the
center of controversy. The mystery he set in motion the day he
left his apartment to venture into the world of George Shippy
was still unsolved and was still helping the newspapers of Chicago sell copy after copy. It would be close to another two weeks
before an inquest was held to determine whether he could truly
rest in peace.

VIII

REPERCUSSIONS

March 9–23

W hile the battle over Averbuch's body and its burial took place in the public eye, a more complicated conflict played itself out within the Jewish community, away from the notice of most of Chicago's citizens. That conflict pitted two competing impulses against one another, impulses as different as the two Chicagos that gave them impetus. On the one hand, many Jews, particularly the influential middle and upper classes, had learned that the surest way to avoid trouble with their non-Jewish neighbors was to share their concerns, to assimilate at least politically. Most such Jews felt pressure to view Averbuch's killing as a political affair best handled by the police and government without interference. As long as the case seemed to be a question of anarchy versus order, Jews could remain safely on the side of order and the American way.

On the other hand, the facts of the affair increasingly suggested that Averbuch had been the victim of, at the very least, a terrible misunderstanding. His having been shot and killed by the chief of police sounded uncomfortably close to something that might have happened to a Jew in Russia. To make matters worse, Schuettler, the acting chief of police, had claimed there would be no investigation of the killing. In other words, the government would not police its own. To Jews who remembered Russia and knew the ghettos of Chicago, the idea that Russian-style policing might gain a foothold in the city was terrifying. In such circumstances they felt compelled as Jews to rally in defense of one of their own.

Virtually all Jews felt pressures from both fronts. A handful responded by defending Averbuch or coming to the assistance of Olga. Many donated money to the fund that Jane Addams had used to hire Hekteon and pay Ickes's expenses. (Ickes had refused payment for his work and asked only for expenses.) Some, like Hamburg the undertaker, donated their services against the general sentiment of the public. Others, like William Nathanson and Miriam Yampolsky, defended Averbuch on political grounds, but thereby sidestepped the question of Averbuch's Jewishness.

Some Jews set out to distinguish Averbuch from the Jewish community as a whole. Some attacked him for his solitary, mad act, claiming he was clearly deranged. Others insisted Averbuch had been driven to the extreme by the inhumane treatment he and his family had received at the hands of the tyrannical Russian authorities. Jews would never become anarchists under just governance, they insisted; Jews in America and Chicago could be counted upon to be good and upstanding citizens. Averbuch was not a typical Jew. Indeed, it was best to forget that he was a Jew at all.

The chief reaction of the majority of Jews was fear: they feared the repercussions from the fact that their community, under whatever conditions, had bred an anarchist, and they feared the uncertainty the affair had introduced to their already marginal situation in Chicago. Not knowing what the affair would mean for them in the weeks and months ahead, they hoped it would simply go away.

There is no way to measure the amount of interethnic violence that grew out of the Averbuch Affair. Jews in Chicago's West Side ghetto were a frequent target of their more aggressive Polish, Greek, Italian, and Irish neighbors, and it would not have taken much provocation to bring about gang attacks or beatings. Such mini-pogroms were a feature of Chicago's West Side until after World War I, when Jewish war veterans, boxers, and gangsters were able to answer inter-ethnic violence in kind.[46] Whether Shippy's claim that he had been attacked by a Jewish anarchist actually precipitated any additional violence is unclear, but no such attacks were reported in Chicago's newspapers.

The sole record of any attacks growing out of the Averbuch affair came from Jane Addams, who felt keenly any violence that threatened the workings of the melting pot she tended. In an address she gave some months after Averbuch's killing, she told of what West Side conditions had been like during the height of the tensions:

> Every member in the colony in varying degrees imme-
> diately felt the result of the public panic. A large tract
> of land near Paris, Ill., which had been negotiated so
> that an agricultural colony of Russian Jews might be
> established, was withdrawn by the seller on the ground
> that the people of the vicinity were not willing to have
> anarchists settle there, although the land was practi-
> cally sold and only the final arrangements remained to
> be completed. The society having the matter in charge
> was forced to give up the entire affair. School children
> were hooted and stoned upon the streets. Inoffensive

young people returning from their work upon the street cars were treated with the utmost contempt. One young man was obliged to leave a dental college because of the persecution of his fellow students, and similar instances might be cited by the hundred. The old anti-Semitic feeling held sway, encouraged and sustained by the anarchy.[47]

It is disturbing, to say the least, that no other publications—even, it seems, the Jewish ones—saw fit to mention such incidents. The full price the Jewish community had to pay for Shippy's story having been widely accepted will never be known.

As Schuettler sought increasingly to downplay the Averbuch affair, it became less and less important for Jewish leaders to distinguish Averbuch from the Jewish community as a whole—the path most Jews who supported Schuettler took as the story broke. Such apologies were necessary only in the face of some accusation; as the accusations died down, the need to clear the entire community diminished. Many Jewish leaders who were inclined to agree with Schuettler either in his refusal to investigate or in his unquestioning faith in the government he served had little left to say.

Among the last prominent Jewish leaders to speak out in support of the police department's position was Rabbi Tobias Schanfarber, a native-born, American-trained Rabbi of Kehilath Anshe Maariv (K. A. M.), Chicago's oldest synagogue and a leading Reform congregation of German Jews. In a widely reported sermon on Saturday, March 9, nearly a week after the killing, he called on the city and federal governments to show "no quarter" to anarchists of any social, ethnic, or financial class. He proclaimed:

> That Averbuch's mind was inflamed by the fiery
> addresses of fire eating anarchists, that he was under
> the delusion that he was still in Russia undergoing the
> tortures of a Kishineff massacre is no excuse for his
> taking the law in his own hands.
>   No man has the right to usurp the law. There will
> be no need for trial in the Averbuch case. He has
> received his just retribution. The fact that some of the
> newspapers have referred to Averbuch as a Jew need
> not make the Jew feel that America is going to attach
> his wrongdoing to all Jews. America is too sane to make
> an entire people responsible for the acts of one man.
>   Judaism and anarchy are antipodal. The Jew
> believes in law. It is one of the charges against Judaism
> that it is law. It believes the laws of God and man
> should and must be enforced. Nothing will please the
> Jew more than the throttling of anarchy of every form.

It is impossible to know how widely shared Schanfarber's feelings were. But, Schanfarber was one of the last prominent Jews to
endorse the idea of no investigation. As earlier commentators had
done, he took pains first to distinguish Averbuch from the Jews
and then the Jews from anarchists. Not stopping there, however,
he took pains to align himself with the police and city administration. Willing to demonstrate Americanness by denouncing any
glimmer of anarchy and calling for anarchists to lose their civil
rights, he could sustain such a position only by insisting on the
difference between Averbuch and the Jews. As other speakers began to acknowledge Averbuch's Jewishness—and gradually to
suggest his Jewishness was a factor in his killing going
uninvestigated—Schanfarber must have found his position increasingly untenable. Within the next few days, no prominent
Jews would echo him.

For the Jews who spoke out in sympathy for Averbuch, the week after the killing marked a turning point. With the publication of Boyarsky's "American Zola" article and the information published by socialist and anarchist presses, it had suddenly become possible to question every facet of the story as Shippy originally told it. Boyarsky's speaking out had been dramatic, but not perhaps unexpected. He was an outsider himself, someone who empathized with the underdogs and the downtrodden. It was rather the speaking out of Zolotkoff, Hirsch, and other more mainstream leaders that marked the gradual taking hold of the position that Averbuch had to be defended as a Jew. Theirs would be the voices that Chicago heard with increasing frequency that second week after the killing.

The same issue of the *Jewish Courier* that had run Boyarsky's article and Zolotkoff's editorial "From Kishineff to Chicago" also ran an interview with an unidentified judge. That judge—almost certainly Julian Mack, one of the most powerful Jewish politicians in the city and someone outspoken enough in his concern to attend the funeral—said he felt certain Averbuch was innocent of any murderous intent. The fact that he made his point anonymously underscores the dual pressures Mack must have felt. As an eminent politician and relatively wealthy man, he had a clear stake as an American and as a Chicagoan. As a Jew, however, he could not but have felt concerned at so apparent an injustice against one of his fellows. Speaking out with the weight of his office but without the openness of his name would have seemed a sensible compromise between the two suddenly conflicting identities.[48]

Similar pressures must have confronted the major contributors to the fund Addams was managing. By March 11, these contributors were still chiefly anonymous. In an interview with the *Daily Socialist*, Ickes noted his group's unease at adding their names to the cause to which they willingly committed their time and money. "We refuse to rush into print with the names of the men connected with the movement for investigation," he said, "till we are sure, as far as may be, of the ground which we are taking. Within the next few days, full announcements will be made."

Those announcements never actually came. The Jewish contributors had already succeeded in demonstrating that there was a strong Jewish sentiment willing to stand up for Averbuch when it seemed a question of standing up for one's Jewishness or keeping quiet on behalf of one's Americanness. The press spoke of "Jewish leaders collecting funds" or "Jewish movements in support of Averbuch." They had little to gain by identifying themselves, except the potential for serious questions concerning their ultimate loyalties.

By March 12, three days after Boyarsky's and Zolotkoff's articles and Mack's anonymous comments, it was clear that the Jewish community was coming to the consensus that there should be an investigation of what took place that morning at Shippy's house. That day, two strikingly different Jewish voices came out strongly with just such a call. Rabbi Emil Hirsch, a mainstream Jewish leader, spoke out at greater length on the affair than he had before, and the *Morning Journal*, a Jewish labor newspaper in New York City, published a vitriolic editorial.

Hirsch came as close to being able to speak for all of Chicago's Jews as anyone could. His Sinai congregation was one of the wealthiest in the city—it included Julius Rosenwald among others—and Hirsch was also active enough with settlement workers and other service organizations to have his finger on the pulse of ghetto life.[49] His remarks were widely reported, including a lengthy excerpt that appeared in the *Inter Ocean*:

> To the number of those demanding full investigation of
> circumstances surrounding the attempted assassination
> of Chief of Police Shippy by Lazarus Averbuch is added
> Dr. Emil Hirsch, pastor of Sinai Temple. Dr. Hirsch
> said last night:
>   There is doubt as to what happened at the home of
> Chief Shippy. I think Averbuch went there for the
> purpose of securing a recommendation from the head
> of the police department, as is required in the country
> he came from. He could not speak English and the
> chief did not know his language. A misunderstanding
> arose. Chief Shippy thought the man was an assassin
> and tried to protect himself, and Averbuch also de-
> fended himself. I did not say, as I have been quoted,
> that there was doubt as to whether the police chief had
> really been wounded.
>   West Side Jews are much worked up over the
> situation, inclining to the belief Averbuch went to the
> chief's house with no evil design. I sympathize with
> them in the position they have taken in demanding a
> full investigation.
>   There is no anarchy among the Jews in Chicago. If
> it is a fact that Averbuch went to kill Shippy, he went as
> a demented man. A man came to my home less than a
> year ago armed with a dagger intent on killing me. I
> turned him over to the police.

Despite its relatively mild tone, Hirsch's statement did create
something of a stir. He would be a more difficult critic for the
authorities to ignore than Boyarsky, although they would do so
all the same.

The *Daily Socialist*, reporting on the statement, interpreted
the closing remarks—about the rabbi successfully having arrested
an intruder at his home—as a sarcastic jab at Shippy, who had
killed Averbuch under similar circumstances. The headline ran,
"Jewish Leader Reflects on Shippy's Courage."

In far bolder language and at far greater length, the *Morning Journal* in New York made a similar claim that same day. Its view of the situation, from half a country away, deprived it of some of the details of the affair but gave it an edge in bringing the entire situation into focus. Under the headline "Shippy Must Prove Why He Murdered Averbuch!" it wrote at length:

> As soon as the first dispatch arrived from Chicago reporting that the "anarchist" Averbuch "tried to kill" the chief of police in his house and was shot by him, we said immediately that there's a bluff here; only one thing is certain—that the Chief had murdered a Jewish young man. Anything further in the dispatch is just Chief Shippy's version and very unbelievable.
>
> Afterwards, at every opportunity, we demanded of Chicagoans that they insist on an investigation.
>
> We are pleased to hear from there that a strong movement has arisen to demand an investigation energetically. A fund of $40,000 is being put together and the services of the greatest lawyers are being arranged for them to work on this matter. Several thousand dollars are already at hand, according to our correspondence.
>
> We support the movement with all our might.
>
> The scandal is unheard of. For all the world to see, a young person lies murdered here and the Chief of Police admits himself that he murdered him. That is all that is clear. Were it another citizen instead of the Chief of Police and were it some dissolute, ignorant, empty aristocrat who could not have been declared an anarchist instead of a respectable Jewish young man—then the usual procedure would have been for the government to consider the householder a murderer, arrest him, and the "burden of proof" would have been laid upon him—to prove that he'd shot the stranger in self-defense.

The government would have officially stood on the side of the victim. It would have brought in charges against the murderer "in the name of the people of the State of Illinois" and the murderer would have had to see about getting his defenders. Were he poor, the state would pay for his lawyer. If he was rich, he himself would have to pay.

Furthermore, as a first thing the dead man would have been brought to the coroner. A coroner's jury would first of all have thoroughly examined the wounds, the murder scene, the persons who were there, etc. so as to get some idea who the guilty party was in this business. When the coroner's jury would have become convinced that there was no question that the victim had come to commit murder, they would have said that in their verdict and the owner of the house would have been set free. But if the coroner's jury would be left even in some doubt, he would have remained under arrest and a trial would have taken place.

That's the legal process as it is supposed to proceed. It's not enough, naturally, that the murderer himself says that the victim was intent on murder. Every murderer could say that. Who believes that? It must be proven!

Now in this land of "equality," what kind of privileged character is a chief of police such that, when he is the murderer, one needs to believe him on his own word—with no further question on the subject, no probing—that the victim of his murder had actually come to murder *him*? Why didn't things go forward in this instance according to the law? Why, with no legal investigation at all, was the Chief's explanation just taken for certain truth, as if one had been there? Why was there a hue and cry in this case not against the murderer but actually against the murdered, against all anarchists, and against the whole labor movement?

Why have Gentile obscurantists been given a chance now to blame all the Jews, and Jewish obscurantists— to blame all the Socialists for the alleged "crime" of a person, about whom right now only one thing is certain, that he's been *murdered*?

Especially when the murderer's story is so unbelievable.

We've already called attention to the facts that show clearly and plainly that the murderer's explanation is a bluff. To this there has been added now the declaration of Averbuch's sister that he, the murdered man Averbuch, had no revolver and no money to buy one.

For the time being, the Assistant Chief of Police Schuettler has declared that there will not be any investigation because "the chief of police needs no defending."

His majesty Kaiser Shippy the First needs no defending. When he says anything, that's final. He is no nobody. His word is sufficient . . . .

Shippy *must* be compelled to prove to a jury his bluff story with which he washes clean his killer's hands!

Given its radical, labor bent, the *Morning Journal* had likely sensed government conspiracies for years in varying situations. The gist of their editorial, though, was that there were inconsistencies in Shippy's story and in Chicago's handling of Averbuch's killing that made a further investigation imperative. That was surely not a radical demand (even if it was stated radically). Whatever false conspiracies it may have decried in the past, the paper's assertions here seemed undeniable and its demand for further investigation reasonable.

The consensus behind such a demand within the Jewish community continued to grow as the days wore on. On March 14, just two days after Hirsch's comments and the *Morning Journal* editorial, the *Inter Ocean* quoted a "prominent Jewish citizen"— quite likely Julius Rosenwald[50]—making a similar demand:

> There is little mystery about this situation if it is only regarded calmly. Doubt has arisen in the minds of a great many as to what happened in the Shippy home, and a number of wealthy Jews have decided to find out the truth.
>
> If the investigation now going on leads to the conclusion that everything in connection with the death of Averbuch was just as has been stated, then we do not care to appear as having challenged the statement of the police or anybody else. If what is discovered in connection with the disinterment of the body and other inquiry is deemed of sufficient import, then the finding of the investigation committee will be submitted at the inquest and legal steps taken to correct any false impressions that have been sent out.
>
> There are no anarchists among the Jews in Chicago and the Jewish race does not wish to submit to the stain "Averbuch, Jew, assassin" unless it is true.

Such a temperate call for an investigation, carrying as it did such implicit faith in the ultimate justice of the government, should not have been challenging. And yet it was. Because Shippy had stated unequivocally what had happened and then Schuettler had supported him with the resources of the police department, any call for further investigation was an implicit questioning of Shippy's honesty and Schuettler's professionalism. It was, effectively, a challenge to the powers that be.

That Rosenwald would have made such a call semipublicly— in a manner that recalls Judge Mack's similar response to the pressures he felt both as a public man and as a Jew—was news, even though he had long been rumored to be one of the chief contributors to the fund Jane Addams was administering. As one of the wealthiest men in the country, he carried a great deal of influence in any affair he chose to enter. Moreover, with his wealth, he represented the third possible avenue to respectability—after the politics represented by Mack and Zolotkoff and the ecumenicalism represented by Hirsch—for Jews. His call for an investigation was a final step: despite the ambivalence and fear that ran throughout the Jewish community, Jewish leaders were effectively agreed in their demand to have the Averbuch affair investigated.

Despite such agreement, there were still a number of questions dividing the supporters of the Jewish community's call for an investigation. Most Jewish observers put their trust in the legal system to ferret out the true story. Others were not so timid, however, and started to propose competing theories in advance of any comprehensive investigation. Implicit in the call for an investigation was suspicion that Shippy might not have been telling the truth; it was just a small step further to propose what the actual truth might have been. That small step evidenced unsettling ideas about the nature of American law and American justice.

Just as his early editorial had played a key role in breaking Jewish silence on the affair, Leon Zolotkoff was among the first mainstream Jewish figures to declare publicly a conviction that the police department was lying. In a statement reported by the *Daily Socialist* on March 14—one that appeared under a headline declaring "Tide Turns and Shippy is Now on Defensive"—he said:

> It is not the characteristic of the race to which
> Averbuch belonged to use a knife. I have studied their
> psychology all my life. I never encountered the instance

of one of them using a knife or dagger—a revolver perhaps—even a bomb. But a knife. Never.

Averbuch may have been an anarchist, but no one about him ever knew it. His mission to the home of Chief Shippy is a mystery today. The police explanation is not substantiated, if it is true. There is nothing of value to prove that he went to kill or for any purpose than to seek a favor.

We do not believe that Averbuch was killed as Shippy says he was. It seems strange that this strong man, this trained policeman, had to riddle a boy of 19, frail and slight, with seven bullet wounds, any one of which would have been fatal. He must have fallen at the first shot. Why the others?

I do not know what happened. But something is being hidden and several persons are lying. As for the dealer who says that Averbuch bought the revolver and knife of him, I am willing to state my personal belief that he has erred. Of that point I am convinced. Averbuch did not purchase the weapons as it is given out he did.

There are many things interesting in Zolotkoff's statement. To begin with, it seems odd at first glance that he would talk of the Jews in the third person. He was a Jew himself, active in Jewish affairs as a Zionist and as a chronicler of the Jewish immigrant experience. As a Chicago politician, however, he especially would have had to avoid what might appear to be the question of dual loyalties. When the facts led him to challenge the story Shippy had told, he couldn't deny them; in challenging it, however, he found it easier to deny his Jewishness.

More to the point, however, is that he was so direct in his accusations. It hardly seems politic of someone in Zolotkoff's position to accuse the chief of police of faking a wound or the police department as a whole of having purchased its main witness's testimony. This was nothing subtle. This was no veiled criticism of the authorities hidden behind a call for the rule of law. This was Leon Zolotkoff talking, the assistant state's attorney. Others would go further.

Just as Zolotkoff's earlier comments had helped set off the call for an investigation that reached near consensus in the Jewish community, so did these statements encourage others to propose assorted theories. Figures as varied as Rabbi Emil Hirsch, Emma Goldman, Louis Post, and Peter Boyarsky would suggest their suspicions about what had taken place both at the time of the shooting and in its aftermath. The most interesting theories, however, would come from lesser known figures and would be broadcast from streetcorner soapboxes and published on letters-to-the-editor pages.

One of the most notable of those letters, from Julius Beresdorfer, of 6328 Ingelside Avenue on the South Side, appeared in the March 21 issue of the *Reform Advocate*, a weekly publication edited and overseen by Rabbi Hirsch. The letter, in its entirety, read:

> To the Editor of the Reform Advocate.
> Sir:—The law of our land holds a man innocent until proven guilty; but public opinion, passing judgment before the law, is more apt in moments of excitement to hold a man guilty no matter how innocent he may be. Most of us allow our judgment to be carried away by the mad current of public opinion, and the reports of a sensational and not altogether reliable press, have already pronounced Lazarus Averbuch guilty far in advance of a judicial inquiry. Some hold him crazy but nonetheless guilty, others claim he was perfectly sane and therefore doubly guilty. A few, more calm and deliberate in their judgment, claim that there is more than one fact in the circumstantial evidence

now before the public that point unmistakably to his innocence. I am one of those few, mistaken perhaps, but perfectly honest and conscientious in my opinion, and I ask if you will not examine with me the foundation on which my conclusion is based.

First of all, as any reader of the newspapers may recall, there was a broad difference in Chief of Police Shippy's account of the tragedy and that which was issued by the press the day thereafter. One of these must be right and one of these must be wrong. Which, then, are we to accept? But dismissing this as something which cannot be gone into at length on account of the lack of space you can allot me, let me proceed to ask several other questions that are vital to Averbuch's guilt or innocence.

How is it possible that a man of Chief Shippy's enormous strength could not hold a boy of nineteen, evidently of comparatively slight strength, by the wrists, after he had the advantage of a firm grip?

If Averbuch went to the Chief's house armed, it is a strong circumstance that points to his guilt. But whose word have we that he was armed? Only the testimony of the Chief of Police. The police have even strengthened their case by insisting the weapons were purchased by Averbuch from one J. F. Corbly, a dealer in weapons in the Chicago Opera House block. But one part of this statement is untrue. Corbly is a pawnbroker and not a dealer in weapons. A dealer in weapons is not a pawnbroker, but a pawnbroker is always a dealer in weapons. The distinction is of the utmost importance, for the simple reason, as every child knows, the power of the police over a pawnbroker is all powerful. They can revoke his license at a moment's notice. To the wise the hint is sufficient.

Shippy had told us that Averbuch stabbed him in the arm-pit. The arm-pit is a fatal spot, and if Shippy was stabbed in the arm-pit and the right arm-pit, how could he have written his report so soon after this wound was received?

Does not the story that Shippy called his wife to search Averbuch's coat pocket for concealed weapons seem just a little bit thin, the Chief's long experience on the police force duly considered? And does it not seem even less plausible that with Shippy's life-long service in the business of this kind that such a long time could have elapsed before he drew his own revolver or before he put it into such effectual—and one might say over-effectual—use? And how about the inexperience of Averbuch getting time, in the face of such a tried and strong adversary, to use both revolver and knife?

Has one single convincing fact been brought forth thus far to show that Averbuch was in any way an anarchist or that he was in any way connected with an anarchist society or group? Certainly not a book found in his house or his trunk was in any way anarchistic. Ibsen's *An Enemy of the People* and Turgenev's *Diary of a Superfluous Man* were seized as contraband. But this simply proves the ignorance of the police and the literary tastes of Averbuch. The other books, without exception, were economic and sociological, not one of them remotely anarchistic. It seems strange that up to date, despite all the efforts to which they sent the whole police and detective force of Chicago, working day and night, [they] have not yet succeeded in finding out that Averbuch had one single friend who was an anarchist or who belonged to an anarchist group.

Averbuch's sister, who from all we can judge, is an honest, simple-minded girl, has said again and again that her brother, insofar as she had the slightest hint, was not an anarchist. Does it not seem strange that if he was carried to such a pitch of insanity by the anarchistic philosophy that he was ready to murder an officer of the law that he would at one time or another have at least discussed the general subject of anarchy with her?

But if Averbuch did not intend to assassinate the Chief of Police, why did he visit his house? His sister has answered that question in a reasonable way and in a reasonable manner. It is the custom of Russian Jews, when they go from one place to another in Russia, to seek first a permit and a "character" from the Chief of Police in the town in which they last resided. Julius Kwint, a Russian Jew and a graduate of the University of Debbtt in Finland, has testified that on the very afternoon of the lamentable tragedy he went to the office of the Chief of Police for such a letter of recommendation and such a "character." Why, in the light of the facts, may we not presume that Averbuch did the same?

There are other extenuating circumstances, some of them minor, some of them major, but enough at least has been said to show that there should be a rigid and searching legal inquiry into the whole unfortunate affair. Chief Shippy ought to be the first to court and welcome it, but his first assistant Schuettler has stated to the press, "There will be no inquiry." Why not? The Jews are involved; the police have done their utmost to prove the Russian Jews a nest of murderous anarchists; let the Jews answer.

I am, Mr. Editor, Yours sincerely,

Julius A. Beresdorfer

Just a day later, the *Jewish Forward*, the New York socialist paper that had been following the case with care, ran an even bolder new theory about the events of the killing. Written in Hebrew by someone identifying himself as Dr. Adam Yisraeli, "Man of Israel," the letter stated:

The energetic work of the *Forverts* in the Shippy case
deserves the deepest gratitude. I wish health and
strength to the hand that wrote those articles, particularly "Indict Shippy!"

Looking deeper, however, into the essence of the
matter, one finds that even our own [side] has assumed
impossible theories, too mild even for the policy.

I am as sure today as on the day after the murder
that only one theory can explain the entire case—a
theory built on the facts and on the tradition of the
Chicago police. The theory can be disproved only if
facts will come to light that no one can now imagine:
What are the cold facts?

1) Averbuch was murdered. Nobody denies that.

2) Averbuch was not an anarchist.

Let's speak openly. We know the anarchists and the
modern maximalists better than the native-born
Americans do. One feature of the anarchist's character
was always prominent, namely:

His deeds—be they good, bad, well-conceived, or a
product of crazy fanaticism—his deeds were always
supposed to be a propaganda means of his ideas!
And that's what they called it, in fact: "Proganda
[*sic*] der That!"

Friends and foes alike must admit then in every
assassination attempt ["*altentat*"], even the unsuccessful ones, the agent always supplied himself with means
to make it clear to everyone that this was not a murder,
but an anarchist action. Everyone, unfortunately,
knows examples of this only too well: Take the craziest
"action" in America, the "action" of [McKinley assas-
sin] Czolgosz. He took care, too, so that it would be
understood that he had done this in the name of
anarchism. Averbuch, however, completely failed to
leave behind a single friend, letter or sign to proclaim
that he had undertaken an "action" in the name of any

ideal whatsoever. That must mean that the anarchist-terrorist Averbuch was content just to kill someone and let the world remain under the impression that this was a plain murder, with no benefit at all for his ideal. Can this be? Only [to] someone totally unfamiliar with the anarchist and terrorist traditions.

3) Shippy did not commit the murder out of fright. Whatever he is, [even] such a physical coward to get scared of a youngster in his own house, to get almost hysterically frightened, for the hysteria to persist for as long as the wrestling had, and at the end be so wild that he begins shooting like a crazy man into the body of that poor young fellow until he's expended all his bullets—such a psychological state in someone like Shippy is impossible.

Don't forget, Shippy is not some poor young fellow. Raised in the free air since childhood, a professional athlete, a giant, he grew up in an atmosphere where delivering a blow to or blackening an eye was an everyday affair. As a policeman, he has to make a specialty of wrestling and fighting, and do you think he could have made it to his [present] position as Chief of Police were he unable? He must also be able to sustain the necessary competition in fist-fighting with all his fellow policemen at every grade for every promotion. At any rate, such a fellow could not have committed the murder out of exquisite terror in the face of the boy.

4) Averbuch didn't go to the Chief of Police in search of "proteksia." That's absurd! He was an intelligent boy. The biggest dummy that comes over has never had the crazy idea to go to the Chief of Police for a proteksia. Just ask among the poorest, loneliest, most ignorant; among the greenest! Where could you hear such an insane idea to go to Binnham or Devery for a "choroshe'eh povodenya"? Besides, it's been said after all that he [Averbuch] himself couldn't write English.

That must mean that he had gone to someone who does know English and does know the country and the other person had written the crazy *proshenya* [petition] to Mr. Shippy. And the other guy also didn't think it was crazy? No, that's too absurd a claim!

Why did Averbuch go to Shippy, into that pirate-nest?

The answer is clear if one looks into the history of the Chicago police. Every institution has its tradition, its customs, its practices. And everyone wishing to become a leader of an institution must first suck up the spirit of those customs and manners.

What is the tradition of the Chicago Police?

Murder and provocation!

Let the reader not think for a minute that I say this just to clear myself and (all of) us from the indirect responsibility, to avoid sharing in the capability for a Jewish embarrassment. Oh no. Had the facts proved that such an illness is present in our movement, then it would be necessary—sooner or later—to look the situation right in the face, analyze it, and try to change it or put it aside. Ostrich tactics—making believe we don't see—that strategy never helped anyone.

As I said, the characteristic tradition of the Chicago police is murder and provocation. I want the reader to understand that [statement] as a report of simple, cold facts.

In our *Appleton's Magazine*—a wealthy, capitalistic monthly journal—there appeared an article last October about the Chicago anarchist trial of 1887, written by a certain Russell.

Russell isn't a revolutionary, God forbid! Twenty years ago he was in Chicago for *The New York World* and sent daily dispatches which, together with other reports, created such a brutal attitude in the whole country against the anarchists that they were murdered and the people [just] smiled.

It is the jewel who is now writing his memoirs of twenty years ago. Each person who reads English and is interested in that subject should consider it his duty to read the articles from start to finish.

In that article, he relates, among other things, that the Chicago police used to surround small groups of workers and break their heads for no cause. If some passerby mixed among the workers, they would half-kill him too. He said also that there was not the slightest legal proof that the famous bomb had not fallen just by accident or was thrown by some madman; that the police brought things that had nothing to do with the events—innocent pieces of iron, glass, lead—and testified that they were "bombs" that they'd supposedly discovered in the possession of anarchists. It also was brought out before the court that *a captain of the police was going around with plans to organize anarchist groups himself so that he could arrest them!* That's not [just] my opinion, it's what the reporter said. And, analyzing these well known facts, I have come to the conclusion *that Averbuch came to Shippy as if to a trap into which a hired provocateur had misled that poor young fellow, with Shippy's knowledge.* And he was murdered there, another thought-out plan.

That is my charge against Shippy. That is the only logical way to explain the bestial slaughter of the unfortunate young man.

And when I see how quickly the entire press threw itself upon the anarchists and socialists; how the murderer and the murder weren't raised as a sensation by the newspapers, even the yellowest, but—as if by mutual agreement—all of them started to make political capital [of the story] in incitements against the labor movement; when I see that, almost at the same moment, Washington responded and began turning the wheels of government machinery with unprecedented speed—then, it seems to me, I see the

traces of the blood of that young Jewish sacrifice
leading to the palace of their majesties Morgan and
Rockefeller and to the offices of their clerks in Washington. It seems to me more or less clear that Shippy,
like Orchard, was only doing the dirty work he had
told him to do. Both Shippy and Orchard will come
out of this not only free but rewarded, because "the
state takes care of those who are loyal to it."
Our work, however, must have another effect! And
it will have! It helps people open their eyes.

Whether Yisraeli's and Beresdorfer's letters were able to con-
vince any of the previously unconvinced is impossible to determine, but they do show how wide-ranging the theories about
Averbuch's death were. They also show how much in disagree-
ment essential allies in support of Averbuch could be.

Beresdorfer, in keeping with the story Olga Averbuch had told,
took seriously the supposition that Averbuch had gone to Shippy's
home seeking a *proteksia* before he departed for Iowa, California,
or some other hope out West. In support of that claim, he mentioned that a certain Julius Kwint, a college graduate, had recently
gone to the chief of police for that very purpose. Yisraeli, on the
other hand, utterly dismissed the possibility. Even the greenest of
immigrants, he claimed, would know better. Even if Averbuch
himself had not known of such a profound difference between
the near police state of Russia and the nominally democratic
America, then surely anyone with whom he had discussed his
plans would have straightened him out.

Each letter writer attacked Shippy's story proper, but with
somewhat different emphasis. Beresdorfer examined Shippy's
claim to have been wounded in the armpit. With respect to his
wound, Beresdorfer insisted, Shippy was simply lying. Yisraeli
ignored the question of the wound, however, and focused rather
on Shippy's claim to have been momentarily over-powered, in-

sisting that Shippy was a well-trained and seasoned fighter. He viewed Shippy's story as preposterous. He misrepresented the nature of police promotion, of course, and probably overestimated the nature and quantity of the fighting Shippy had been called upon to do in his youth and career and so weakened his argument, but his central point remained an echo of the question Shippy's earliest critics asked: How could Shippy not have handled Averbuch? Why did he have to pump bullet after bullet into someone apparently so little a physical match for him?

Each addressed the ideological questions of the affair differently as well. Beresdorfer harked back to the point that the police were unable to find any evidence linking Averbuch to the anarchist movement. Aside from the few socialist-tinged popular works, there was no evidence pointing toward Averbuch's political beliefs. Yisraeli sidestepped the question of Averbuch's affiliations and speculated instead on Shippy's motives. He spun out a seemingly far-fetched plan that would have drawn the poor young immigrant into the chief's home where he could be killed in order to legitimize the government's planned crackdown on anarchism and immigration. Such a hypothesis demanded accepting a well-developed conspiracy theory, but inasmuch as it was an attempt to explain the politics that surrounded the killing, it is worth noting.

Despite their different emphases, Beresdorfer and Yisraeli would likely have embraced one another's claims. Each one was arguing, after all, for Averbuch's innocence in the face of overwhelming physical and political force. Each shared the same essential feeling that Averbuch had been a victim; that whatever had driven him to Shippy's home that morning was something ordinary and naive. Their shared task was to clear his name from the false and ubiquitous stories against it. They were setting out, as Yisraeli concluded, to "open the eyes" of the public to the injustices done to a poor, defenseless immigrant.

Nevertheless, their differences probably tell us more about the difficulty of their task than their agreements tell us about how widely accepted their theories were. Reconsidering those differences—over such issues as whether Corbly's testimony was worth disputing, whether Averbuch had actually written out a petition to Shippy that was covered up, or whether Averbuch's actions were identifiably those of an anarchist—it seems clear each writer set out to answer different charges. That is, each chose a different emphasis in defense of Averbuch because each imagined Averbuch accused of different things. Was he really an anarchist? Was he perhaps a wiry, strong athlete? Was he an impossible naif? Was he armed? Was Shippy an instigator or a dupe? Beresdorfer and Yisraeli who like Ickes, Goldman, and Addams were in the thick of the debate, did not agree on which of those many questions to address because they too were metaphorically overwhelmed—overwhelmed, that is, by the headlines and photographs of the popular press.

Averbuch's supporters found themselves in the near impossible position of having finite energy in the face of a wild, speculative newspaper world that saw itself as having told the story and was ready to move on. It had taken almost two weeks before Shippy's initial statement received the kind of scrutiny that finally broke it down. There simply weren't time and resources to mount the kind of public debate that the many charges against Averbuch would require. For all that Beresdorfer, Yisraeli, and other writers and observers may have reconsidered, probed, and ranted about the case, their words would never amount to more than a small aftershock to the explosion of speculation against Averbuch in the first few days after the shooting.

As the coroner's inquest neared, the Jewish community looked toward it with mixed emotions. It would be the first public, official forum in which Shippy's use of force would be considered.

Shippy would have to answer at last for having shot Averbuch as many as five times. On the other hand, it would not be a trial. No one would consider Shippy's fundamental guilt or innocence, merely the appropriateness of his having used lethal force. The hard-won consensus that further investigation of the case was warranted still held, but there were murmurs about whether the inquiry represented sufficient investigation.

On March 17, five days before it published Yisraeli's letter, the *Daily Forward* had printed an editorial boldly titled "Indict Shippy." Beginning with a lengthy review of the facts still in question—a review that Beresdorfer and Yisraeli accomplished more dramatically—it went on to call for criminal charges against the chief:

> Shippy has shot and killed Averbuch. If he has done so in cold blood or in an excess of groundless cowardly terror, it is murder. If he has committed the act in protection of himself against an actual danger, it is justifiable manslaughter. Which was it in fact?
>
> Whenever one man kills another it is customary in a civilized community to apprehend the slayer and to institute an investigation into the facts surrounding the killing. Why is Shippy not apprehended? Why do the Chicago authorities not investigate the killing of Averbuch?
>
> It is true, Shippy asserts that he killed the boy in self-defense, but since when do civil authorities accept the bare statement of the slayer as conclusive proof of his innocence? It is true, Shippy is a high police official, but since when do police officers enjoy the legal privilege of killing at discretion?
>
> It is true, Averbuch was but a poor foreigner, but when does the law openly recognize the distinction between the sacredness of the life of the poor foreigner and that of a wealthy citizen?

Suppose a high police official were shot and killed in the house of a workingman and the latter claimed that he committed the deed in self-defense. Would the authorities of Chicago take his mere word for it? Or has the dread sound of the word "anarchism" such a tonic effect on the rulers and pillars of society as to turn them into a howling, frantic, terror stricken mob devoid of all sense of reason and justice?

If anarchism stands for arbitrary violence and wanton disregard of the rights and lives of one's fellowmen, then it is the conduct of Shippy and Chicago authorities in this case that constitutes real anarchism; an anarchism all the more dangerous and dreadful for the fact that it is supported by the vast powers of organized government, and practiced by the very men whom the people have chosen to preserve law and order.

The hopes of the *Daily Forward* could not begin to carry the influence that a grand jury would, of course. No one was about to indict Shippy and charge him with murder, let alone with anarchist organizing. Yet the editorial does indicate some of the restlessness that Jews felt over the upcoming inquiry.

Louis Post, not a Jew himself, spoke even more directly to the matter in a brief editorial in the *Public* on March 21, just four days before the inquiry was scheduled. He wrote:

"We are ready to accept the verdict of the coroner's jury as it is, if the rest of the community is willing to abide by it." These are the measured words of *The Jewish Daily Courier*. They should sink deep into the minds of the whole people of Chicago. Is the rest of this community willing to abide by that verdict? In the interest of the due administration of justice let us hope not. If the proceedings before the coroner's jury are fairly re-

ported, the investigation was a farce, having no other
apparent object than the exoneration of the policeman
who killed the boy; and unless the grand jury probes
this case to the bottom, with neither the fear that seems
to have paralyzed the Chicago bar nor the favor that
seems to have influenced the coroner's investigation,
human life may be regarded in Chicago as a matter of
small concern when it is a policeman who kills.

Despite being eloquent as always, Post was also (as he so often
was) in the considerable minority. Few people would echo his
and the *Forward*'s call; most of the rest of Chicago had simply
had enough of the Averbuch Affair.

Chicago's Jews in particular appeared content to abide by the
verdict of the inquiry. There were no public meetings, protests,
or parades. They were deeply conflicted. As Jews they felt obli-
gated to defend one of their own; as Americans they felt compelled to call for institutional justice. Their main hope was that
the affair would simply go away. Eventually falling in line behind
the call for an investigation, they were not interested in pushing
that demand much beyond what the police and city government
were willing to grant them.

As the coroner's hearing approached, therefore, it was already
growing less and less relevant to the general public. It would still
be a forum for questions many had demanded that Shippy,
Schuettler, and the others answer, and it would still be an opportunity for the media to review the affair and the questions of anarchy; but its chief appeal increasingly seemed to be that it would
mark the end of the affair. It remained of vital importance to a
handful of people, Olga Averbuch, Jane Addams, George Shippy,
and Harold Ickes among them, but to many others it promised
the possibility of forgetting about the incident altogether.

IX

THE AFFAIR GOES NATIONAL

CONGRESS QUARRELS AND EMMA FINDS A LOVER

March 2–23, 1908

If the fate of Lazarus Averbuch and the fortunes of Olga Averbuch were of diminishing interest to most of the public, the fear of anarchy that Averbuch's killing helped bring to the fore remained not just a local, but a national concern. Civic and religious leaders and politicians at all levels cried out against the curved-backed, shadowy, foreign-born anarchist capable of murder most foul against society's pillars for no reason anyone could understand. It did not matter that a growing body of evidence suggested Averbuch had not been an anarchist; the specter, once raised, proved an effective political totem. If the details surrounding the Averbuch Affair made it an increasingly cumbersome source for anti-anarchist fervor, no matter; the shadow it cast was consistent with the near panic the very word *anarchist* caused.

One key to the stereotype of the anarchist—as the type was sketched in editorial cartoons, public nightmares, and the earliest versions of the official story of what happened in Shippy's home that fateful morning—was that he was a foreigner from eastern or central Europe. Never mind that, until the assassination of President McKinley by Leon Czolgosz seven years before, the best-known anarchists in America had all been of British, German, or other Western European descent: A. R. Parsons, Sam Fielden, August Spies, and the other leaders of the Haymarket Square demonstration; Bill Haywood and other founders of the IWW (Industrial Workers of the World); and intellectuals such as Proudhon from France or aristocrats Bakunin and Kropotkin from Russia. Still, the image of the anarchist as Italian, Hungarian, or Russian-Jewish held. Such ethnic groups, with markedly different languages and cultures, terrified many Americans simply by dressing differently and by carrying on a noisier commerce; how could their growing numbers, then, not be disturbing? And how could their equation with the powers of anarchy not be natural? The campaign against anarchy often proved to be a veiled campaign against foreigners in general; driving out the foreigner would drive out the anarchist.[51]

The main front in the campaign against foreigners was the battle over reforming the longstanding U.S. policy on open immigration. As early as the turn of the century, federal lawmakers began proposing restrictions on immigrants who were felons, socialists, or anarchists. In early 1907, the debate had flared up again with the introduction in Congress of an immigration reform bill and with the gradual cresting of American nationalism that took place under President Roosevelt's direction. What had been a more or less theoretical argument took on a human face in February 1908, however, with the assassination of Father Heinrichs in Denver and a month later with the Averbuch incident. With the priest and the police chief as victims of alleged anarchists, the congressional debate grew more intense, the federal executive branch got more involved, and local witch-hunts intensified.[52]

On February 20, 1907, Congress passed a law prohibiting, among other things, known anarchists from immigrating to the country. Using the word *anarchist* in Section 2, it spelled out the concern more fully in Section 38.

> That no person who disbelieves in or who is opposed to all organized government, or who is a member of or affiliated with any organization entertaining and teaching such disbelief in opposition to all organized government, or who advocates or teaches the duty, necessity, or propriety of the unlawful assaulting or killing of any officer or officers, either of specific individuals or of officers generally, of the Government of the United States or of any other organized government because of his or their official character, shall be permitted to enter the United States or any territory or place subject to the jurisdiction thereof. That any person who knowingly aids or assists any such person to enter the United States or any territory or place subject to the jurisdiction thereof, or who connives or conspires with any person to enter therein, except pursuant to such rules and regulations made by the Secretary of Commerce and Labor shall be fined not more than $5,000, or imprisoned for not more than five years, or both.

There was little genuine reason to single anarchists out for such specific penalties—they constituted a much smaller percentage of the socialist, revolutionary left wing than public fear would have it—but Congress did nonetheless. That they did so further underscores the correlation then between anarchy and the larger issue of immigration.

On March 2, 1908, a little more than a year after the immigration law was passed and the very day Lazarus Averbuch found himself confronting George Shippy's gun, the House of Repre-

sentatives took up a bill that would have modified the law. Proposed by Congressman William Bennet of New York, the bill
would have empowered the government to deport any resident
alien who, before becoming a citizen, committed a felony. Its
strength, argued Bennet, was that it would rid the country of "a
number of criminals that we can well afford to lose" as well as
"deter aliens from committing crimes in this country." Its flaws,
retorted Illinois Congressman Adolph J. Sabath from Chicago,
were twofold: the term *felony* was interpreted differently in different states and the law would punish after the fact. "Think you
that laws are just, that laws are righteous and fair which would so
severely punish a man by imprisonment and subsequent deportation because he has stolen, perhaps, something of small value,
while we allow to go unpunished men who are guilty of stealing
millions of savings of the people, thereby causing unspeakable
suffering and hardship," he said in a lengthy address before Congress.[53] Ironically, he uttered those words within an hour or two
of Averbuch's killing. (Philip Bregstone, in his history of Chicago's
Jews, claims Averbuch was killed even while the Congressman
spoke.[54]) In a vote taken under suspension of the rules, the bill
failed to get the necessary two-thirds majority, but it did receive a
simple majority of the votes cast: 64-50.

On each of the following two days—the first when news of
Averbuch's killing would have been available to Congress—the
affair was mentioned in the *Congressional Record*. On March 4,
two days after the killing and the bill's defeat, Bennet had read
into the congressional record articles from the *Washington Post,
Chicago Tribune, New York Sun*, and other newspapers across the
country that dealt with the affair and its early ramifications. The
extent of the documentation—on a subject in principle only tan-
gential to the bill Congress had already dismissed—bespeaks an
obsession by Bennet, if not by others in the House as well.

But Bennet continued. Later the same day, he attempted to reintroduce his bill. In the discussion that followed, he responded to Sabath's spirited opposition:

> We have got the remedy in our hands to diminish criminality among the aliens in this country, and I call the attention of my friends from Illinois to the fact— not in gloating, because what happened in Chicago on Monday may happen in New York City today, and worse—that on the very day when they and some of my own colleagues from New York were opposing and voting against that bill an alien who had been in the country less than three months went to the residence of the chief of police in the city of Chicago and shot his son, attempted to shoot the father, shot an assistant, and was himself killed by the chief of police. . . . The man had not committed any crime in Europe. He had not admitted the commission of any crime, had not been convicted of any, so far as I am advised, and therefore had a right to stay in this country.[55]

Bennet's point was that if Averbuch had lived, he would of necessity have been permitted to remain in the country. There was no mechanism for deporting an alien without a criminal or radical political record who subsequently committed a crime in the United States.

Although Bennet's request for a second hearing failed, the sentiment of ethnophobia inspiring it remained evident throughout the time the Averbuch Affair was in the limelight.[56] Congress considered and rejected a bill that would have limited the number of Chinese and Japanese immigrants the country would accept. On March 19, Representative Henry D. Flood of Virginia read before the House of Representatives a resolution the House of Delegates had passed a month before. Entitled the "Joint resolution to oppose in every possible manner the influx into Virginia of immigrants from southern Europe," it read:

> Resolved by the Senate of Virginia (the house of delegates concurring), that our representatives in both Houses of Congress be, and they are hereby, requested to oppose in every possible manner the influx into Virginia of immigrants from southern Europe, with their Mafia and Black-Hand murder societies, and with no characteristics, to make them, with us, a homogenous people, believing, as we do, that upon Anglo-Saxon supremacy depend the future welfare and prosperity of this Commonwealth, and we view with alarm any effort that may tend to corrupt its citizenship.

As shockingly hateful as such a statement is, Flood added to it his personal feelings:

> Practically all the immigrants who came to this country before 1880 were from northern Europe. They were of Celtic and Teutonic origin; or, I might say, they were of the strong historic peoples, the authors of the civilization of northern Europe—of the land of Shakespeare and Gladstone, of Emme and Burke, of Goethe and Bismarck.

> Would that we had gone at this wholesome pace; that we had not gone into the recesses of "all sorts and conditions of men" to meet the immediate clamor of hustling, a restless and a feverish age.[57]

The Virginia resolution and Flood's remarks were greeted with applause.

The following day, March 20, just five days before the much anticipated coroner's inquest into Averbuch's killing, the House took up yet another bill aimed at keeping undesirable immigrants out of the country. Proposed by Representative Everis A. Hayes of California, but with the support of the indefatigable Representative Bennet, the bill would have permitted either side—the government or the applicant—to appeal an immigration board's decision. On the surface, such a bill would seem to have offered unsuccessful applicants an opportunity to challenge decisions keeping them out of the country. With the tenor of recent discussions, however, it seemed yet another safeguard against admitting immigrants who were criminal or subversively political. As Representative James R. Mann of Chicago put it, "It would be rather hard on some poor fellow who wants to be a citizen when, after the court has passed on it in his favor, the government may take the question up on appeal."[58] For procedural reasons, the bill never came to a vote.

In the twenty-two days the House was in session between Averbuch's killing and the coroner's inquest, it took up or made mention of immigration issues on seven different occasions. Averbuch's killing and reputed motives were national concerns. Little of the most hateful legislation proposed during the three weeks was passed, but one wonders what lasting impact the specter of Averbuch as the swarthy anarchist assassin had on Congress. That members of Congress were aware of him in light of Shippy's original story is obvious; how much his image contributed to what would be a subsequent fifteen-year trend to increase immigration restrictions is, of course, impossible to tell.

Outside of Congress, the federal executive branch was also busy. Secretary of Commerce and Labor Oscar Straus served as point man for anti-anarchy efforts possible within the existing laws. With the strong backing of President Roosevelt, he proposed unprecedented cooperation between immigration officials and local law enforcement officials to single out and prosecute anarchists. How successful they were in their efforts remains in dispute, but they made clear through their attempts that they feared anarchists every bit as much as Representative Bennet did. Straus reacted to the Averbuch killing almost immediately. As the first Jew ever to hold a U.S. cabinet position and also the son of a man who had fled from Germany to escape political reprisal, he may have felt some affinity with Averbuch. As a successful American businessman and politician, however, he must have felt pressure to adhere to a high standard of American orthodoxy. On March 4, two days after the shooting, he came forward with his much publicized directives calling for cooperation in running "alien Anarchists and criminals" out of the country.[59] In his memoirs, Straus claimed the timing was only coincidental, that he had been preparing them for some time before the assassination of Father Heinrichs and the Averbuch Affair. He wrote:

> The exclusion and deportation of criminals and
> anarchists was another phase of the immigration
> service to which I had given considerable study. I found
> the law provided for arrest and deportation of criminal
> aliens only up to three years of the time of their
> landing, and that there was gross misconception
> regarding the scope of the law. There was no coopera-
> tion between our immigration officials and the local
> police departments for the detection of such persons.
> The police departments of most of our cities were
> disposed to assume that by virtue of the immigration
> law the whole subject fell under the jurisdiction of the
> Federal Government; and on the other hand our
> officials did not confer with municipal officials to make
> use of the immigration law. It is one thing to provide
> for the exclusion of criminals and anarchists, but it is
> quite another to discover, on entry, whether a person
> belongs to either class. They are usually neither illiter-

ate nor lacking in cunning and deception, but within
three years they may be detected, as "birds of a feather
flock together."

I decided to issue a circular to all commissioners of
immigration and immigration inspectors, with a view
to bringing about cooperation with the local officials. I
took the subject up in the Cabinet and the President
approved. It so happened that while this circular was
being prepared, an Italian immigrant, recently arrived,
killed a Catholic priest in Denver while the latter was
officiating at a mass in his church, and a day or two
thereafter another recently arrived immigrant, a
Russian, attacked the chief of police of Chicago and his
family with a dagger. Both of these men would have
come under the deportation of the immigration law
had the police been aware of these provisions, as in
both instances that had been suspected, by their
affiliations and their talk of being anarchists, as that
term is defined in the Immigration Act of February 20,
1907. Under the local criminal laws this suspicion was
not enough to justify arrest.[60]

Other officials echoed Straus's concerns. It was difficult to determine a would-be immigrant's background on the strength of a
brief interview and whatever documents he or she had from the
old country. The executive branch very much wanted a bill
like Bennet's to go through, but it would be several years before any did.

In the meantime, however, immigration officials claimed
some success. Robert Watchern, commissioner of immigration,
told the *New York Times* on March 4 that his office had turned
back hundreds of criminal or anarchist petitions the year before.
"Last year we sent back three hundred of these criminals, which
is a much larger number than a few years ago. But if we had the

necessary law they would go back in thousands." Most of these three hundred were fugitives from justice, whom the various consuls general had advance information about. Echoing him, Representative Bennet claimed immigration officials were turning back as many as fifty a month.[61]

The term *deportation* was being thrown around in two distinct ways, however, and the confusion around that term obscures just how successful federal efforts were. There was little dispute over the government's power to refuse residence to any aliens it could determine in advance were fugitive criminals or probable nuisances. At times, then, *deport* meant turning away such unwelcome applicants once they had arrived at Ellis Island or one of the smaller debarkation points. As a result, Straus, Watchern, and Bennet could indeed claim they had deported hundreds of anarchists and criminals. It is not clear how many of these deportations occurred at the time of the Averbuch Affair, although the *Morning Journal* reported that twenty-four-year-old Abraham Bashek, whose "single sin is being an anarchist," had his permission to immigrate repealed between March 5 and 12 while he was detained by immigration officials.

At issue in Congress, however, was whether someone who had already achieved resident alien status could be returned to his or her native land. The word *deport*, then, referred at times to a more dramatic government power. The government's best-known attempt to use that power in the wake of the Averbuch killing came when a federal magistrate in Chicago approved the extradition of Christian Rudovitz, a revolutionary, to Russia in early 1909 on the basis of an extradition demand by the Russian government. Jane Addams reported a wave of panic throughout the Russian-Jewish ghetto, where residents feared they would not be safe once the U.S. Government acquiesced to the extradition sought by the Russian government. On later appeal, Rudovitz's extradition was revoked by Secretary of State Charles Root.[62] The government seems to have failed as well in its efforts to deport a few anarchists who had been resident aliens for less than three years: a Belsky from Brooklyn, a Gotken from Philadelphia, and an Erlich from Boston.[63]

Because of the dual meaning of deport, Straus and other officials never needed to acknowledge that they failed in their efforts to rid the country of any anarchists already United States residents. (Years later, after World War I, the United States would deport Emma Goldman and Alexander Berkman and other anarchists, but that was a different issue and one long off.) That they did manage to turn away a number of fugitive criminals seems incontrovertible, but how many legitimate anarchists they prevented from entering the country can never be known. That they likely spent disproportionate resources on the cause in relation to the result they obtained seems clear from the vantage point of more than eighty years later, but it speaks to the endemic fear the government and many citizens had of what they considered the shadowy and the foreign.

At the same time that Straus and Congress were doing what they could to rid the country of anarchists, the country's most famous anarchist continued trying to find a place where she could speak about the Averbuch Affair and about anarchy. Emma Goldman was not a woman easily deterred from anything, and she was not about to quit her search for a podium in the face of efforts to the contrary by Herman Schuettler and the Chicago police department. Following the collapse of her plans to use Ben Reitman's Brotherhood Welfare Association meeting hall as the site for the March 14 lecture, she and her band redoubled their search.

Compounding their difficulties, however, was the undeniable attraction developing between Goldman and Reitman. Each was a veteran political organizer, skilled and focused enough to do her or his work even with the distraction of a blossoming romance. However, each had also worked in a very different movement than the other. Goldman's associates would distrust Reitman throughout their ten-year relationship, tolerating him only for her sake. Reitman's hobos, for whose sake he had been both self-promoting impresario and genuine agent of comfort, would soon take the symbolic step of stripping him of his hobo kingship, declaring his conduct "unbecoming any member of the hobo party" for consorting with "Emma Goldman, the Anarchist Queen."[64] Even the hobos considered the anarchists no better than felons.

Rebounding from the initial setback, the anarchists devised a plan to have Goldman speak unannounced at a meeting where a substantial group of potential sympathizers would be gathered. Schuettler and his men, perhaps having good intelligence reports, perhaps guessing well, or perhaps leaving no opportunity untried in harassing Goldman, determined to tail her any time she attended a large meeting. On March 16, a pair of detectives tailed her to 75 Randolph Street, where the relatively obscure Anthropological Society was holding its weekly meeting. They called for backup and then went into the meeting hall as the first of the police officers on the scene. Within the next forty-five minutes, a total of sixty officers would arrive, turning the audience into a sea of blue. The meeting became a spectacle—Reitman took the opportunity to introduce an "unemployed dog"—despite its rather tame location in downtown Chicago. Hulda Potter-Loomis, an active and vocal anarchist, spoke on the evils of medicine as a science. Although the text of the speech has been lost, all accounts agree that it was boring beyond necessity—boring and apolitical. It ended three hours later and then only at the request of an audience member.

Newspapers made fun of the police for the pointless show of force. The *Daily Socialist* ran the headline, "Heroic Feat Performed by Shippy's Men: Fifty Policemen Listen to Three-Hour Lecture on Medicine; Emma Goldman There." Goldman herself commented:

> Really, I didn't intend to speak. I simply came to hear Mrs. Loomis's masterful address. It was beautiful, wasn't it? They have lovely policemen in Chicago, haven't they? Funny so many of them are interested in anthropology. I'm sure everybody is glad to see so many of them at the service.
>
> You know, the loveliest boy has been following me ever since I came to Chicago. On the way down this afternoon I stopped to have my shoes shined, and he rushed away to a telephone. I knew right away we would have a good escort by the time we got here. I'm particularly disappointed not to see Mr. Schuettler. He's sick. I am going to send him some flowers. I think every officer in Chicago who is not sick is here.

That round went to the anarchists.

The next evening showed that the conflict between Goldman and Schuettler was not in fun, however. It pitted a woman committed to acting on her social beliefs against a man who had dedicated his life to upholding the laws she challenged. On March 17, assuming perhaps that the police would not dare to swarm a second consecutive meeting, Goldman and her party arranged for her to take the podium at a meeting that evening to deliver an address called "Anarchy as It Really Is." Hoping to break the invisible blockade that had kept her from speaking throughout the course of her Chicago stay, they kept their plans to the tiny coterie around Goldman—including Chicago movement members Miriam Yampolsky and William Nathanson. The only outsider they confided in was Reitman, presumably at the request of Goldman.

Goldman had only just managed to take the stand, however, when she was dragged from it by Police Captain Mahoney, leader of the squad tailing her. Mahoney reportedly told her, "You should realize now that we regard you as a trouble maker and a nuisance and will not tolerate you." She replied, "Is that so. Well, I know how to be a lady though you don't know how to be a gentleman . . . the time will come in this country when I shall do as I damn well please." The assembled crowd nearly rioted when she was dragged from the stage. It took a few words from Goldman and the cool head of Nathanson to calm things.

Later that evening, when Goldman and the other planners of the event met to determine what had gone wrong with their secrecy, Reitman failed to join them. He would later say he had been arrested and then was too occupied to make the meeting. Circumstantial though it was, the evidence pointed to his having betrayed them. He had been the only outsider aware of the plans, and now he had not bothered to meet with them. Goldman, confused, didn't know what to think. For his part, Reitman told the *Morning Journal* that he and Goldman had arrived at an "affinity" with one another.

Under terrific strain from her conflict with the police, her constant moving from house to house, and her uncertain relationship with Reitman, Goldman suffered a physical collapse. It turned out to be inconsequential and she recovered immediately, but it bespoke the pressure-cooker Chicago had become for her.

Still determined to prove that Chicago could not keep her from speaking, Goldman nonetheless had to leave the city for a brief time in order to fulfill prior speaking engagements in Milwaukee, Winnipeg, and Minneapolis. The suspicions against Reitman she found herself battling were fanned during a farewell dinner they held at a popular restaurant. She wrote in her autobiography:

We were a gay party, making merry in the last hours of
my strenuous Chicago stay. Soon Ben arrived, and with
him came a heightened mood.

Not far from us sat a group of men, one of whom I
recognized as Captain Schuettler, whose presence
seemed to me to pollute the very air. Suddenly I saw
him motion towards our table. To my amazement, Ben
rose and walked over to Schuettler. The latter greeted
him with a jovial: "Hello, Ben," familiarly pulling him
down to his side. The others, evidently police officials,
all seemed to know Ben and be on friendly terms with
him. Anger, disgust, and horror all mingled together,
beat my temples, and made me feel ill. My friends sat
staring at each other and at me, which increased my
misery.

Ben Reitman, whose embrace had filled me with
mad delight, chumming with detectives! The hands
that had burned my flesh were now close to the brute
who had almost strangled Louis Lingg, near the man
who had threatened and bullied me in 1901. Ben
Reitman, the champion of freedom, hob-nobbing with
the very sort of people who had suppressed free speech,
who had clubbed the unemployed, who had killed poor
Overbuch [*sic*]. How could he have anything to do with
them? The terrible thought struck me that he might be
a detective himself. For some moments I was utterly
dazed. I tried to eliminate the dreadful idea, but it kept
growing more insistent. I recalled our social on March
17 and the treachery that had brought the police and
reporters to that gathering. Was it Reitman who had
informed them? I, who had been fighting the enemies
of freedom and justice for nineteen years, had exulted
in the arms of a man who was one of them.[65]

Away from Reitman and the city for several days, she would refuse
to read his communiques and determined to break off with him
altogether.

During her time in Chicago, Goldman faced pressure from more than just Schuettler, the police, and Reitman. As a foreign-born anarchist, she appeared for a time as if she might be someone Secretary Straus's federal cooperative venture would make it possible to deport. Since she had been in the United States for twenty-three years, had married a U.S. citizen, and had a home, she was secure, however. Speaking with apparent disappointment to the *Inter Ocean* on March 18, Schuettler said, "I am almost sure now that her exile could not be accomplished under the law. She is a lecturer and author, and not a vagrant. So long as she has a home she is privileged to remain here. In fact, the police acted with unwarranted haste Monday night when they removed her from the platform at Workingmen's Hall. She had a right to speak there. If she tries again to lecture in Chicago, she will not be disturbed provided she appears in a proper place." That promise of a respite came, however, just as she was readying to leave the city, although she still vowed to return.

On a comparable though distinct front, Schuettler and Coroner Hoffman turned to a controversial source for more information about the still largely mysterious past of Lazarus Averbuch: they contacted the Russian government. Although the results of their inquiry were reported to have arrived in Chicago on March 17, they made no comment on them, filing them away for the time of the coroner's inquest. Rabbi Emil Hirsch spoke for many in the immigrant community when he commented on the request:

> The Chicago police have as good a chance to get a correct report on Jesus Christ from Satan as they have of getting a correct report on a Russian Jew from the Kishinev police.
> The Russian police are interested in proving that every Russian Jew who escapes murder at their hands is

an anarchist and a menace to any country he enters. The Kishinev police in all probability will report that Averbuch, who was 15 years old at the time of the Kishinev massacres, was an anarchist of the deepest dye, that from his cradle he was engaged in the making and throwing of bombs.[66]

In general, though, the request was carried out without attention, and it became a sheaf of documents in the growing pile Hoffman collected in preparation for the inquest.

For anarchist groups across the country, the Averbuch Affair produced, ironically, some benefits in the face of the increased persecution they felt from the government and angered citizens. The notoriety brought on by Averbuch's and Goldman's constantly being in the news helped swell attendance at speeches and boost sales of anarchist literature. In Detroit on March 15, a large socialist meeting—during which Shippy was denounced—culminated in the arrest of a local union official. The formerly dormant Chicago chapter of the National Organization of Anarchists in America pledged to raise $20,000 toward purchasing a meeting site so they would not be subject to the arbitrary blackballing they had seen Goldman suffer. In Milwaukee, on her tour away from Chicago, Goldman reported unprecedented audiences and encouraging sales of her books and magazines. It would be a short-lived revival; except for the coming peak of the anarcho-syndicalist IWW just before World War I, there would never be a significant anarchist movement in the United States again.

It was in Minneapolis, on the last leg of her tour away from Chicago, that Emma Goldman finally softened in her opposition to Ben Reitman. He had written and cabled her almost constantly when she was away, claiming by telegraph that he had fallen in love with her and couldn't understand why she wouldn't see him. She had ignored all the messages except one, to which she cabled back, "Do not want love from Schuettler's friends." Her love-hate was rooted deeply. A good deal of her unquestioned strength as a speaker and social activist grew out of the passion she felt for her work and toward life in general. She was a woman out of her time when it came to issues of sexuality. She was an early activist on behalf of birth control and championed free love and sexual freedom. She believed in the power of the unfettered individual: unfettered by government, unfettered by philosophy and tradition, and unfettered by circumstance. She must have seen immediately in Reitman, who was the embodiment of spontaneity, the dark possibilities of such beliefs. He would demonstrate in their eventual decade together how living without restraints could sometimes mean being shockingly insensitive to those close to him. He would show her more than once that appetite was not an admirable substitute for conscience. But he would also show her more passion than any love—save politics—that she would ever have.

Finally Reitman joined her in Minneapolis. As she wrote in her autobiography:

> Ben's explanation of the Schuettler scene swept my
> doubts away. It was not friendship for the man or
> connexion [sic] with the police department that had
> made him known to them, he said. It was his work
> among tramps, hobos, and prostitutes, which often
> brought him in contact with the authorities. The
> outcasts always came to him when in trouble. They
> knew and trusted him and he understood them much
> better than the so-called respectable people. He had
> been part of the underworld himself, and his sympa-
> thies were with the derelicts of society. They made him

their spokesman, and as such he frequently called on the police to plead in their behalf. "It never was anything else," Ben pleaded: "Please believe me and let me prove it to you." Whatever else may have been at stake, I had to believe in him with an all-embracing faith.[67]

In the midst of the stepped up prosecution of anarchists and immigrants, against the advice and wishes of their different sets of friends, and in the middle of the Averbuch Affair, they had found each other. It would be a turbulent next ten years for each of them.

X

THE INQUEST

March 24–25

The week leading up to the coroner's inquest of Chief Shippy's shooting of Averbuch was comparatively uneventful. Emma Goldman was out of the city for much of the time. Many others who had commented on the case found it increasingly convoluted and decreasingly useful as a soapbox subject. Those in the city hoping to use the incident as a spur to crack down on anarchy found it frustrating that the case linking Averbuch to an anarchist conspiracy had broken down and somewhat baffling that the boy's correspondence failed to turn up any concern with political philosophy. Those hoping to support free speech and political tolerance had their hands full with Goldman's public escapades. Those wanting to defend the hapless young Jewish immigrant had had their say and, in general, feared pressing the matter so far as to be mistaken for anarchists themselves. There were many still anticipating the inquest—the hearing room would be filled beyond capacity even after those who could not prove a connection to the case were denied admission—but at bottom it concerned two families: the Averbuchs, with Olga Averbuch and her circle of supporters and advisors, and the Shippys, with their domestics and colleagues.

March 24 restored the affair to front-page headlines for the first time in at least a week. "Inquest in Averbuch Case: Promise of Full Inquiry" announced that morning's *Tribune*, and the *Daily Socialist* noted, "Will Lift Veil on the Averbuch Tragedy at Inquest Today." With the inquest getting underway at last, the hope of some sort of resolution to the affair won back the interest of many of the curious and disaffected. The affair had dragged on for close to a month, raising as it went several uncomfortable questions all around, questions that threatened to impugn the police, the Jewish community, and the anarchist community. It was time for it to be over.

In essence, the inquest put on trial the story that Shippy had originally told the press. If the evidence demonstrated that Shippy had indeed shot Averbuch in self-defense, prompted by legitimate suspicions of Averbuch's intent, then he would be exonerated. Since the only witnesses to the shooting itself were the Shippy family and their bodyguard, Foley, it was unlikely anyone would challenge the thrust of the story. But there were still questions: Had Lazarus Averbuch really been an anarchist? Had he been armed when he went to the Shippy's that morning? If so, was there evidence he had actually intended to kill Shippy? What role had Harry Shippy, the chief's son, played in the doings that morning? What was the nature of Shippy's wounds? What had happened and in what order that morning? Since coroner Hoffman would act the part of a grand jury—not determining guilt or innocence but rather making the legal determination whether a full-scale trial and inquiry should take place—the only real question was whether the inquiry would go on or end.

Harold Ickes would later describe Hoffman as a "typical, cheap politician" who was "always looking ahead to the next election."[68] Hoffman's patron, of course, was Mayor Fred Busse, the final word

Fig. 14. Lazarus Averbuch inquest.
Photograph: *Chicago Daily News.* Chicago Historical Society. DN–006106.

in party affairs. Busse's most visible appointee was Shippy, and
any inquest verdict that cast aspersions on Shippy would, naturally enough, reflect back on Busse. During the inquest, Hoffman's
role would be central. Not only would he serve as judge, but he—
along with the six-person jury—would be the only person au-
thorized to put questions to the witnesses. Not even Ickes—there
to represent the Averbuchs' interests—was supposed to be able
to ask anything.

The cards, as it were, were stacked against the immigrants.
The Averbuchs did have two edges, though. First, because of the
public scrutiny the inquest would be under, they could be assured that there would be no glaring impartialities in its conduct. Hoffman would go so far as to break with practice and
permit questions from interested participants—notably Ickes and
Schuettler—although such occasional questions would still fall

short of cross-examination. Second, with Ickes, the former newsman, working on their behalf, they had an ally well equipped to
follow any backroom dealings that might take place. As the inquest readied to begin that morning of March 24, no one could
predict how far it would probe.

A total of twenty-eight witnesses crammed into the space of
a single day told and retold accounts of that morning and of what
they knew of Lazarus Averbuch. The ultimate plausibility of
Shippy's story rested on two legs: that things that morning had
happened as he said they had and that Averbuch had actually
intended to kill him. Since Foley, the Shippys' maid, and the entire Shippy family were witnesses to the shooting itself, the inquest focused on that leg of Shippy's story.

As the events of that morning unfolded themselves before
the jury, none questioned the fact that Averbuch had arrived at
the Shippys' door at approximately 9 A.M. and rung the doorbell.
Shippy's daughter Georgietta had answered the door, and
Averbuch had told her "I want to see Chief Shippy." She had then
called her father, who ignored the envelope Averbuch proffered
him and, instead, grasped him by the wrists and called on his
wife to search him for any weapons.

What was the envelope? Hoping there might be some clue to
Averbuch's mission in it, Hoffman brought in a handwriting expert, Warren Drake, to determine whether the script of Shippy's
address had been written with the same hand that had written
several postcards seized from Averbuch's room. Drake said yes,
Averbuch had addressed the envelope himself. Olga Averbuch,
while acknowledging the postcards as her brother's handwriting,
said otherwise. The envelope's address had been written by someone else, she said. Since the testimony of three witnesses—Shippy,
his daughter, and investigating officer Captain Danner—agreed
that all the envelope contained was a blank piece of paper, nothing came of the discrepancy.

The way Shippy had held Averbuch while his wife searched the boy for weapons was another curious matter. It seemed unlikely that a man of Shippy's size—over six feet tall and weighing 2l0 pounds—would be unable to restrain the much smaller Averbuch. In Shippy's words, though, the story made sense:[69]

> As the man handed me that letter there overspread his face the most vindictive look that I ever saw upon a human countenance in the thirty-two years that I have served the city.
>
> I let the letter fall. I grasped the man by both wrists and edged him along the hall, shouting at the same time to my wife, "Mother, come here and see what is in this letter."
>
> Then I noticed something about his garments that made me think he was armed, and I said as my wife came up: "See if he has a gun." She proceeded to search him and said, "Yes, he has!" He began kicking my wife, and I edged him along under the stairway and pushed him against the telephone stand. I released him a moment and he came at me with a knife in his uplifted left hand.

In response to a juror's question, Shippy added:

> He was strong enough to wrest himself from my grasp. It is difficult to hold a man by the wrist. There is not a man in this room who could hold me in that manner.

And, when asked by Ickes whether he had struck Averbuch, he said:

> No, I held him by the wrists. My intention was to get his gun, but if I had succeeded he'd have disembowelled me with his knife.[70]

It all seemed straightforward enough. Why a police officer of Shippy's experience would not have attempted a more secure hold on the boy is a question no one raised, but in general it seemed plausible that Shippy would not have been able to hold Averbuch down. Despite the widespread conjecture that Shippy's story was patently unbelievable, he was able to make it stand up.

And yet, there was one key question—Shippy's wound. After Averbuch had kicked Mrs. Shippy, the story went, he had struck Shippy with his long knife, narrowly missing a fatal spot just under the arm. Blood had flown everywhere according to early reports, and Shippy had released his hold and staggered back. Early critics of Shippy's story had wondered how the chief, so wounded, was able then to file a report on the incident within hours. Anticipating such criticism, Hoffman called on Dr. Albert Goldspohn, a physician, as an expert witness. His claim that he had found a small knife wound under the chief's arm, one considerably inflamed, indicating a contusion, went unchallenged.

When Hoffman called on Mrs. Shippy to produce the shirt her husband had worn when he was stabbed, the courtroom was in for a surprise: the white shirt was virtually unstained. In the words of the *Daily News* correspondent, there were "marks of a few clots." Mrs. Shippy explained that the woolen shirt underneath the white shirt had been saturated with blood, but had inadvertently been thrown away. The one she held had been thrown into the laundry, where it was accidently washed the following day before anyone thought it might be necessary as evidence. How such an unlikely series of accidents jibed with Shippy's own testimony that he was "in my shirt sleeves with my vest on" was a question no one thought—or had opportunity—to ask.

The story continued: After Averbuch had shaken off Mrs. Shippy and stabbed Chief Shippy, Harry Shippy came charging down the stairs to defend his parents and grabbed the arm in which Averbuch held the knife. Harry's testimony of his involvement was moving and effective. Pale and weak from his wound and days in recovery, he had to be escorted to the stand by his sister and a nurse from the hospital, where he remained under supervision. In a "clear and steady" voice, according to the *Inter Ocean*, he reported:

> Averbuch pulled his revolver as I held the hand in which he clutched the knife. The gun was a few inches away from me. I saw the flash, and felt the bullet plow through me. Just then Averbuch dropped his knife and turned his attention to my father again. I went into a back room after I told Papa I had been shot, and lay down on a couch. I saw the blood on my father's shirt, where he had been stabbed, and saw him shoot once after I had been shot.

At one point as he spoke, Harry tried to raise his arms to demonstrate how he had held Averbuch's hand. When he did so, a spasm of pain shot across his face. Later, when he exited from the courtroom, he nearly fainted and had to be caught by his nurse and sister. No one dared question the authenticity of such testimony.

Shippy himself resumed the story with what was surely the most dramatic part of his lengthy testimony:

> My son, who came running downstairs at this time, grabbed [Averbuch's] right hand. Then I heard a shot, and my son gasped, "Papa, I'm shot!" Then I ceased to be a police officer. I was a father. I shot three times as quick as I ever pulled a gun in my life. I don't know where I shot him, but every bullet found its mark.

It was a compelling defense: his attack on Averbuch had been one of a blind urge to protect or avenge his son. Again, there was little one could say in the face of such testimony.

The end of the story came quickly: the shot allegedly fired by Averbuch drew Foley, stationed out front, into the house. Arriving just after Shippy's three shots had staggered Averbuch—shots that would prove later to have been lethal—Foley grabbed at Averbuch's gun hand. But, just as Averbuch had proved too slippery for Chief Shippy and too cunning for Harry Shippy, he had one last trick for Foley. Pulling the trigger one last time, he shot Foley through the hand. Foley, in response, fired two more shots and Averbuch collapsed.

Foley, who sat with his arm in a sling, reported that Averbuch's revolver landed at his feet after he collapsed and dropped it. In a calm, unhurried way, he explained that he had not seen the bulk of the struggle, just the final moments in which he was involved. Ickes would later acknowledge that Foley had been the most impressive witness for Shippy. "He had a story to tell and he stuck to it," Ickes wrote.[71]

We can't know what would have happened if Ickes had cross-examined witnesses to the scuffle and shooting itself. As the *Jewish Courier* would point out, "The eye witnesses to the tragedy are all members of Chief Shippy's household, and only they and God knows the truth, and God has not appeared as a witness at the inquest." Someone with an interest in seeing Shippy exonerated would have had to go against that interest to tell any story that might have implicated him in murder. Therefore, the first leg of Shippy's story—preposterous as it still seemed that a pinioned boy could draw and strike with a knife so quickly, that he could stave off Harry Shippy with one hand and shoot another, and that, fatally wounded three times, he could still shrug aside Foley's lunge and shoot him—stood unchallenged.

The second leg of Shippy's story, however, had witnesses aplenty with no personal stake in Shippy's future. Lazarus

Averbuch, most of them claimed, was simply not the sort of person who would set off to assassinate a police official. He was frustrated, certainly, at the obstacles he confronted. He was even attracted to social causes. But he was at heart exactly the sort of immigrant the country would want—hard-working, reasonably bright, and full of dreams.

The first witness to testify to Averbuch's character—in fact the first witness of the inquest—was the only one in the entire country who genuinely knew him, Olga. Olga Averbuch made a sympathetic figure as she wore black mourning clothes and walked into the courtroom leaning on the arm of her nurse. The *Daily News* described the scene:

> Like a scared deer, Olga Averbuch came into the crowded room, and testified as the first witness. Her face was pale, her walk was weak, but her eyes were clear and steady as she entered the room.
>
> Calmly she took the seat directly in front of Coroner Hoffman, Harold L. Ickes, her attorney, and assistant Chief Schuettler.
>
> Once when her gaze turned in the direction of attorney Ickes she looked Chief Shippy squarely in the eyes and there was a suppressed trembling of her lips as if stifling emotion.
>
> She was dressed all in black with a veil of mourning on her black hat. From behind her spectacles shone a pair of eyes that disclosed the depth of her recent suffering.
>
> "What is your full name?" asked Coroner Hoffman.
>
> For a moment Olga Averbuch hesitated as if dazed by the surroundings. The nurse who had led her into the room and who stood at her side, gently stroked her and leaned over to encourage her to answer.

"Averbuch," she answered in a whisper.

"Your first name?" said the coroner in German—
"Your full name, please."

"Olga Averbuch," she replied in clear tones.

"You are the sister of Lazarus Averbuch, who is
dead, are you not?" said Coroner Hoffman.

"His name was not Lazarus," replied the young
woman.

"By what name was he known? What was his
name? What did you call him?" asked the coroner.

"Jeremy and Harry," replied the witness.

"What is the translation of Jeremy? Is it not
Lazarus?" asked Coroner Hoffman.

"I have a small brother named Lazarus, but he is
alive," said Olga Averbuch.

For all that had been written and speculated about the young
immigrant from Kishinev, this was the first time the public learned
that his first name was not Lazarus.

Olga's testimony, dramatic and moving as it seems to have
been, lost some of its effect by coming so early in the day. Moreover, without cross-examination, Ickes was unable to use her to
bring out issues that might have opened the case up to broader
inquiry. No one raised the issue of Olga's allegedly having been
"sweated," a fact that might have led into an inquiry about the
generally overzealous investigation of the affair. No one raised
questions of Averbuch's family background that might have established the improbability of such a person being predisposed
to assassination. And, with the bulk of the accusations against
Averbuch coming later in the inquiry, Olga could not refute them
directly.

One claim that Olga did deny was that her brother had frequently contemplated suicide in the weeks before he went to
Shippy's house. Under direct questioning from Hoffman, she said

her brother had never told her he was considering killing himself and that she had never told anyone he was. W. H. Eichengreen, Lazarus Averbuch's employer and Olga's benefactor, claimed later in the day that Olga had told him on a number of occasions that her brother was discussing suicide. There was no way to resolve the word of one witness against the word of another, so the only conclusion one could take from the conflict was the suspicion that Averbuch might have been deeply depressed.

Eichengreen's claim certainly deserves some consideration; he was a friend and supporter of Averbuch. He had known Averbuch better than anyone not living in the West Side ghetto and he had good things to say about the young man in his testimony:

> Averbuch worked for me for three weeks as a hustler. His sister had been employed by my wife as a seamstress. She told me that her brother was out of employment and had come home one night and she had heard him and another man discussing suicide unless they could obtain suitable employment.
>
> She told me that Averbuch had said he didn't want her to work her fingers off and that rather than steal he would do away with himself. This excited my sympathy and I tried to get a job for him. I failed, so I employed him myself at $6.00 a week, although I had no need of him.

There is no reason to doubt Eichengreen's claim that he hired Averbuch more out of compassion and affection than for genuine business needs. He and his wife had befriended Olga and seemed throughout the affair to be concerned with her welfare.

Yet, even in his claim that Averbuch had been depressed, he was careful to link that depression to Averbuch's dissatisfaction with his opportunities in America. It was Averbuch's essential commitment to the American goal of working hard and making a better life for oneself that had impressed Eichengreen enough to give Averbuch a job. He went on in his testimony, then, to undercut what might have seemed briefly a potential cause for Averbuch to have gone to the Shippy household in search of the chief's and his own death. Eichengreen said:

> A large commission dealer from Iowa had agreed to employ Averbuch and was to have taken him away on Tuesday, or the day following the shooting. I tried to interest Averbuch in his future.

With such an employment opportunity in or near his grasp, Averbuch would seem not to have reason to continue as morosely as before. However depressed he had once been, he looked to be growing more hopeful right at the moment he was killed.

The mystery about the Iowa job offer remained, however. What Olga had to say about any such offer on the day of the inquest has not been recorded, but in earlier comments—most notably the letter she dictated to the *Jewish Daily Courier* staff— she claimed not to know of any firm offers her brother had had. It seemed likely, of course, that Averbuch had been pursuing possible employment zealously, but it would be hard to believe that he planned anything so significant as to leave Chicago without telling his sister.

The testimony did clear up at least one of the lesser mysteries around the incident. Richard Dreger, a salesman who worked next door to Eichengreen's egg-packing plant, claimed that Averbuch had come to him on the Friday or Saturday before the shooting and asked him to point out Shippy's address in the telephone book. Dreger had written the address for him on a slip of paper, the same slip found later on Averbuch's body. Although Dreger also said he had overheard Averbuch asking a coworker about Emma Goldman's upcoming speech, his testimony established almost nothing new; he could not say why Averbuch had gone to Shippy's home, but only that the young immigrant had been thinking about going for at least a few days before the incident. The key testimony intended to determine why Averbuch had gone there came from J. F. Corbly, the pawnbroker who claimed to have sold him the knife and gun allegedly found at the scene. Schuettler had felt during his investigation—and Hoffman seemed to have agreed with him—that, if he could prove Averbuch had purchased the weapons only days before he went to Shippy's, then he could prove that Averbuch had intended to harm the chief.

Calling Averbuch a "country jake," Corbly unveiled a ledger that indicated Averbuch had bought the weapons on February 29 at about 4:00 P.M. According to the records, Averbuch had claimed to be twenty-five years old and had given his address as 216 Washburne Avenue. Identifying the police exhibit as the weapons he had sold, he went on at length about his memory of the sale:

These are the weapons that I sold him on that date. Here are my private price marks.

Averbuch came into the store alone and a saleswoman sold him the revolver for $8 and I sold him the knife for $1.75 and the box of cartridges for 40 cents. He beat me down 75 cents on the whole purchase. He looked like a country jake, and I thought he would get in trouble before he got home because he stuck the gun in his outside coat pocket.

I asked him what he was going to do with the weapon. He said: "I'm going back to Europe, and I want to fish and hunt." I asked him why America was not good enough for him.

He said he did not like it in this country and that he was going back to Germany on Monday. I tried to sell him a smaller knife and he said no; he wanted the bigger one.

"What kind of English did he use?" Ickes interrupted.

> Broken English. Didn't seem to know where to get
> off at. He stuck the gun in his pocket and went down
> the street with the shaft of that—knife sticking out
> under his coat, and I remarked to my clerk:
> "The police will seize him before he's gone a
> block."

For people attacking the testimony, it was hard to know where to start. Since, in separate testimony, Eichengreen's foreman Miller had testified that Averbuch had remained at work the day of the alleged purchase until 4:30, there was a problem with the time of the purchase. Corbly insisted Averbuch had bought the weapons between 4:00 and 4:30, so it became his word against the Eichengreen company, the validity of his ledger against the timekeeper's record book.

The choice—if there had been opportunity in the inquest to force one—should not have been difficult. The Eichengreen company stood to gain nothing by reporting Averbuch had stayed late; it would need, in fact, to pay him for that time. Corbly stood to gain—so his critics charged—the favor of the police department by supporting them in their case. Eichengreen's was a large company, employing numbers of people both as management and as labor. Corbly ran a small shop, with only one cashier working under him. That the large company's books would need to be accurate and that the small one's could easily be altered should have been clear.

Ickes made some attempt to undermine Corbly's testimony. He asked him to confirm that his business was indeed a pawn shop, intending thereby to establish how susceptible he would be to police pressure. Corbly bristled, crying, "Do you want to insult me?" Hoffman knew better than that. "Everything in that book's as straight as a string," he said. Unable to challenge him with the fact of his being widely known as a pawnbroker, Ickes tried another tactic: he asked Corbly to describe some of the other customers whose sales were recorded in the ledger. At this, Hoffman grew angry, saying he would permit only such questions as were material. After a brief protest, Ickes yelled out, "I shall not ask any more questions." Corbly went on to answer the question of his own volition, but Ickes had no opportunity to follow up.

The result of it all unquestionably hurt any slim chance Ickes had had of sending the investigation to a full-fledged trial. Corbly, whose testimony was the only third-party indication that Averbuch intended violence against the chief, was clearly the most impeachable witness of the lot. Under adequate cross-examination, he would have been hard-pressed to retain his credibility. With his testimony effectively unchallenged, the police case against Averbuch was complete. Shippy's claim to have acted in self-defense was secure.

The inquest was as notable for what it did not include as for what it did, however. Since Hoffman was the only one permitted to call witnesses and the only one unfettered in his questioning, he had wide discretion in the topics he would permit the jury to hear. Issues he did not consider material—or that he had reason for excluding—simply weren't considered.

At no point did anyone address Olga Averbuch's ordeal. Neither Schuettler nor his lieutenants were asked to justify their lengthy questioning of her—she had been held for close to seventy-two hours without charge, had been "sweated" under intense interrogation, and had been shown her brother's corpse in an effort to shock a confession out of her. It may well be true that such questions would not have related directly to the question of

Averbuch's doings or intentions, but, if Ickes had had the opportunity to mount a full defense, he would undoubtedly have used the police's sloppy drive to uncover the story they wanted as a keystone. Schuettler had known from the start what he would find and, with the exception of coconspirators, he found it; that process—leaving in its wake as many inexplicably jailed witnesses as it did—smelled rotten.

More directly to the questions of the inquest, no one determined what exactly was true or untrue of the rumors that Averbuch had planned to leave Chicago. Eichengreen testified that Averbuch would be leaving for Iowa within days. Corbly said Averbuch had told him he was returning to Germany. (No one else seems to have made any mention of such a plan.) Rumors persisted that Averbuch had some plans that would take him to California. Yet Olga Averbuch, the person who could have been expected to know more about his plans than anyone else, seems to have had no idea her brother was intending any move at all.

If Ickes had been able to establish that Averbuch did indeed have employment waiting for him somewhere outside Chicago, it would have bolstered his defense considerably. Not only would an impending job have taken away Averbuch's purported main motive, it would have supported the main explanation Averbuch's supporters suggested for his having gone to the chief's home in the first place. He went, many suggested, in order to obtain a certificate of good conduct like those required of people moving from one town to another in the Russia he had known before coming to the United States. His supporters claimed Shippy would have seemed the logical one to ask for such a certificate.

If Averbuch had indeed gone to Shippy's in search of a letter of good conduct, it would have cleared up one more of the big mysteries in the case: the meaning of the blank paper he had folded into the envelope he held in his hands when he knocked. It might well have been that he wanted Shippy to write or sign something on that paper. Some observers considered the possibility that the envelope had originally contained something else, something that might have undone the entire Shippy story, but there seemed to be no evidence that the envelope held anything but the blank paper.

The most remarkable element absent, or largely absent, from the inquest was something that had been at the heart of Schuettler's investigation from the very beginning: the issue of Averbuch's anarchism. Considering that Shippy and Schuettler had immediately labeled Averbuch's motives as political and that they had had the police force ransack every known anarchist center in the city for some indication of a conspiracy, the question was treated in the slightest of ways during the inquest.

Beyond Dreger, the only witness to mention anarchy was John Shannon, a fellow employee of Averbuch's at Eichengreen's. Asked whether Averbuch had ever told him anything about Goldman, Shannon replied at length:

> Yes, the first part of the last week he worked he asked me if I knew that Emma Goldman was coming here to speak.
> "No," I replied, "She isn't coming here. They won't let her speak here."
> "Who will stop her," he asked. "She has been in this country twenty years. They let her speak in Boston and Philadelphia. Will the chief of police stop her?"
> I told him I didn't know as the chief of police would prevent her from speaking, but the government would.
> "Where does the chief of police live," he asked.
> "I don't know," I replied. "Somewhere on the north side." I told him that the government at Washington had notified the police here not to let Miss Goldman speak. Then I said to Miller who works with us: "Miller, this fellow is an anarchist and they are going to

send him and Emma Goldman back to the old country." Of course, I was just joshing.

Then I told Averbuch, who was always complaining because he wasn't succeeding as he thought he ought to, not to worry—that he was young and would get along all right. He said Rockefeller has all the money there is in this country and asked me what I would want him to do—like they did in Philadelphia, where the anarchists had some trouble? I said, "nothing like that!"

He told me that Emma Goldman was to speak here on March 5, that he had seen the handbills advertising her appearance.

It would certainly be farfetched to determine from such testimony that Averbuch was a committed anarchist. Despite the interest Shannon reported Averbuch to have in hearing Goldman speak, he more clearly indicated how naive the young man had been about political affairs. Indirectly, Shannon told the jury that Averbuch had known virtually nothing of anarchy.

Given the bent of the investigation, one would have anticipated that Hoffman would pursue the anarchy connection more fully. Without it, after all, Averbuch would not seem to have had any motive for attacking the chief. Averbuch had never had any personal dealings with Shippy, and he had had no encounters with the law in his time in Chicago. Yet, Hoffman simply let the matter fall.

Why Hoffman, Schuettler, and Shippy would have let such an issue go by without playing it up would have remained a mystery if not for Ickes's explanation of his strategy years later. In his unpublished memoirs, Ickes explained what he had hoped to accomplish at the inquest, where he would have to operate without cross-examination privileges and without the power to call witnesses.[71] His main concern, he said, was to refute the claim that Averbuch had been an anarchist. Nothing would bring the boy back to life, he reasoned, but removing the charge of anarchy would make it more possible for Olga Averbuch to lead an unharassed life and might well diffuse some of the tensions under which the Jewish community labored.

Unable to pursue that goal directly, Ickes had used his inside expertise. During the second autopsy, the one conducted by Dr. Hekteon, Ickes had noticed irregularities. He discovered, on pressing Hekteon, both that Hoffman had neglected to restore Averbuch's brain after the first autopsy—a fact the newspapers would never uncover—and that Hoffman had missed a fatal wound, one from a bullet that had struck Averbuch in the back. It would have been impossible for either Foley or Shippy to have shot him in the back if the story they had told were true in every particular. Ickes then met with Hoffman, familiar to him from his newspaper days, in private. He reported that conversation in his memoirs:

> Then I said, "Coroner, I hope that you don't intend to let the police go on the stand and fill up the record with a lot of talk about anarchy?" In a blustery way, he said, "I am going to let the police put in whatever evidence they have." I replied that of course the police ought to be allowed to put in all the *evidence* that they had, with emphasis on the word "evidence," but I argued that the police had no evidence of anarchy or of Averbuch's connection with any anarchistic group. To permit them to charge, without a shred of evidence, that Averbuch was an anarchist merely in an attempted justification of what had happened at Shippy's house would be unfair and a rotten thing to do. Blustering more than ever, Hoffman insisted that the police would be allowed to say what they pleased about anarchy.

I kept myself in perfect control, but at this point I remarked quietly, "Well, Coroner, if we are going to open the case wide, let us put in all the evidence that we have. I would like you to ask some questions about Averbuch's brain." Hoffman's jaw fell wide open. It was clear that he knew about this incident. "You want to beat me for re-election, do you?" he asked. I inquired how putting into the record the facts about Averbuch's brain could have any possible effect on his re-election. His answer was: "You know very well how the Orthodox Jews carry on if even so much as a drop of blood is lost. All the Jews in Chicago would vote against me if they knew that the brain had been taken from the body for examination at the Presbyterian Hospital." I replied that I had no interest except to see that justice was done; that if the police could prove anarchistic connections I was willing that they should be permitted to prove them, but that I did not propose to allow Averbuch's name to be smeared in defense of Shippy. Hoffman said that he would talk the matter over with Herman F. Schuettler, Assistant Chief of Police.

I arrived at the Coroner's offices in the County Building the next morning about fifteen minutes before the time set for the opening of the inquest. Peter Hoffman was nervously awaiting for me in the hall. He clutched me eagerly and took me into his private office. He said, "There won't be any talk about anarchy at the inquest." My reply was, "The police have no evidence that Averbuch was an anarchist, have they?" His answer was "no." The authority he gave was Schuettler.[73]

Although we must certainly take Ickes's report with a grain of salt, his explanation does account for the curious absence of anarchy in the inquest testimony. The only two people who would ultimately have cared whether Averbuch was a murderer were Averbuch and his sister. But the entire Jewish and political communities would suffer if he were labeled an anarchist. With Averbuch dead and his sister under the guidance of Jane Addams and others interested primarily in preventing the killing from inciting ghetto violence, there was no one to protest Ickes's backroom deal.

How much Ickes's account of the deal is after-the-fact justification is difficult to tell. Since he was clearly in a situation where he could not win the inquest, he might have constructed a story that permitted him to look back on his part in the affair as somehow pivotal. There is no reason to doubt that he met privately with Hoffman—but it does seem unlikely that a political animal as seasoned as Hoffman was would cave in to Ickes's threats as smoothly as he reports. How much influence Hoffman would have had with Schuettler, a notoriously shrewd man, is also in question.

Whether the deal, in whatever form Ickes was able to perpetrate it, was a good idea at all is another difficult question. If he had been able to extract some public recognition from Schuettler—or at least Hoffman—that there was no evidence Averbuch had been an anarchist, then he might have won something. As it was, none of the newspapers covering the inquest noted the surprisingly little attention the issue of anarchy received in the different testimony. Moreover, most later commentators on the case continued to refer to it as an instance of anarchy. Whatever actual victory Ickes managed to pull out of the inquest was slim indeed and certainly of dubious comfort to Averbuch's ghost. Ickes would admit in his memoirs to still owning the extra bullet Hekteon had discovered.[74] That bullet, never introduced into evidence and resting for years in a drawer, seems an apt symbol for the deal.

It came as no surprise to anyone, then, when the coroner's jury delivered its verdict that afternoon. The statement read:

> We, the jury, find that Jeremiah Averbuch, also known as Harry Averbuch, came to his death while en route in a police ambulance conveying the deceased from 31 Lincoln Place to the German Hospital, 754 Hamilton Court, from gunshot wounds, said wounds inflicted by bullets fired from a revolver held in the hand of George M. Shippy and a revolver held in the hand of one James Foley in the residence of said George M. Shippy, 31 Lincoln Place, on the morning of March 2, 1908.
>
> And, from the testimony presented, we, the jury, believe the said shooting was justified and exonerate George M. Shippy and James Foley from blame.

That was it. The inquest was over and, in the eyes of the law, Shippy was free and clear of blame in the Averbuch shooting. Shippy and his family would have to confront the incident as individuals, and Olga Averbuch would have to mourn for the rest of her life the brother who never did find his piece of the American promise. But most onlookers could, and would, put the entire affair behind them. Ickes could later boast in his memoirs that in his first case as a lawyer he had been successful in keeping the "anarchist" label off Averbuch, but in complying with the ground rules of the coroner's inquest, Ickes, the lawyer, made it possible for Chief Shippy to leave the hearing a vindicated man— and Averbuch was branded forever as an attempted assassin.[75]

XI

MAKING SENSE OF
IT ALL

THEORIES ABOUND
March 4–30

It was not that easy to slam the lid on the Averbuch case, however. The inquest may have marked the formal and public end of the affair, but it could not put to rest the suspicions that had been bred by a month of accusations by and against the competing interests in the Jewish community, the various socialist and anarchist groups, and the police and city government. There was too much animosity in the air for everything to die down at once and on schedule. In a way comparable to the Haymarket Affair, although decidedly smaller, it would linger as an unresolved flareup between the two Chicagos that generally coexisted without surface violence.

As a result, after the Averbuch Affair had left the front pages of newspapers, after it ceased to be a burning issue for social leaders like Jane Addams or Emma Goldman, even after it was no longer a fresh wound to the Shippy or Averbuch families, the questions of what actually happened when Shippy shot Averbuch and why Averbuch had gone to Shippy's home in the first place persisted. Participants and observers of the inquest and investigation would continue to put forward their speculations in the coming weeks, months, and, eventually, decades, but no one would ever successfully explain all the story's inconsistencies. The Averbuch Affair remains a mystery, but it certainly does not want for theories about just what happened and about just what it represents.

One reason the case is so little recalled today, despite the great stir it raised, was that another "anarchist outrage" stole its thunder soon after the inquest had ended. On March 28, 1908, in New York City's Union Square, the police broke up a proposed Reitman-like gathering of the unemployed. Having dispersed the would-be demonstrators, the police remained on the scene intimidating any further troublemakers. They made a good target, however, or so thought an inept, or at least unfortunate, nineteen-year-old Russian immigrant named Selig Silverstein. As he readied a bomb to lob into the midst of the police, Silverstein miscalculated, and it exploded in his hands. A bystander was killed, and Silverstein was maimed beyond recovery.

Silverstein, it turned out, was unambiguously an anarchist. He told investigators (he would live almost two weeks in terrible pain) that he was frustrated at not being able to find a job and that he believed in anarchist doctrines. He carried a card identifying himself as a member of the Anarchist Federation of America, and police found in his apartment a number of fund solicitations from Emma Goldman's old cohort Alexander Berkman. He was the immigrant-anarchist-assassin nightmare come to life.

Because of the obvious similarities to Averbuch, the Silverstein incident at first resurrected fears of an anarchist reign of terror. Both men were Russian-Jewish immigrants, although Silverstein, who had come to the United States in his childhood, could hardly be called a "greenhorn." Both had seemingly been incited to their deeds after taking part in marches of the unemployed, and both were presumed to be the dupes of better-educated anarchists or the instruments of anarchist cabals. Silverstein seemed initially to be as much New York's Averbuch as Averbuch had seemed Chicago's Guiseppe Alia, the assassin of Father Leo Heinrichs in Denver in February 1908.

The similarities in the case soon fell apart. Where Averbuch's motive and life were subject to wide interpretation, Silverstein was alive to announce his creed. There was little call for investigation in Silverstein's case, although the New York police responded with a general harassment of left-wing activists that rivaled the efforts of Schuettler. Silverstein could serve unambiguously as an anarchist bogey man; Averbuch, for all that had been written and said of him, remained too much of a mystery to be an effective symbol.

Observers would try to link the two cases along with the assassination of Father Heinrichs—and indeed they are often written of together in histories of the period—but the chief effect of the Silverstein incident seems to have been to dampen interest in the yet unanswered questions about Averbuch.[76] Schuettler commented on the Silverstein case that it was "enough to justify us for putting a stop to public demonstrations of this sort." In so doing, of course, he did no more than insist that the Averbuch case was as cut-and-dry as he had first claimed; that it was, in essence, the Silverstein case and not the thorny Averbuch Affair.

Silverstein was easier to confront than Averbuch. President Roosevelt would use the case as the impetus for his widely distributed statement on anarchy (appearing in the April 10 issue of the *New York Times*), in which he proclaimed:

> When compared with the suppression of anarchy, every other question sinks into insignificance. The anarchist is the enemy of humanity, the enemy of all mankind, and his is a deeper degree of criminality than any other.

The Silverstein case would also prove not to have the same power the Averbuch Affair had had in drawing larger crowds to anarchist rallies or in selling more anarchist literature. It was not divisive, just frightening. By the end of the first week of April 1908, Averbuch's name had practically vanished from the American press.

Before word of the affair disappeared altogether from the press, however, it experienced a final gasp as the different newspapers and magazines offered comments on the proceedings of the inquest. While mainstream newspapers limited their reaction to reports of the events through the eyes of their correspondents, the more liberal publications didn't hesitate to condemn the proceedings. There were too many unanswered questions for everyone to rest quietly.

The *Jewish Daily Courier* had a brief editorial ready for its March 25 issue:

> At the coroner's inquest over the body of Lazarus Averbuch the jury returned a verdict that the killing of the unfortunate Kischineff youth was justifiable. We recognize that, under the circumstances, no other verdict could have been expected.... As far as we are concerned, we may feel satisfied with the verdict. The loss of a young life, with all its chances to become useful to itself and to others, is under all circumstances a thing to be deplored. But doubly painful was to us the cry that Averbuch was an anarchist. We felt all the injustice which the false alarm of an "anarchist plot" was bound to cause to thousands of our people, both here and abroad. According to the testimony of all those who knew Averbuch, we have lost in him a respectable, intelligent and hard-working boy, and we have lost him under circumstances which are tragic as

they are mysterious. We regret his untimely death and console with his family. But we were much more deeply affected by the suffering of thousands which was likely to be caused by the unwarranted imputation of anarchist plots. The inquest has established the fact that Averbuch was no anarchist; that he was a peaceful, intelligent boy who worked every day and attended night school almost every evening. The inquest proved that he had no connection with anarchists. This was the point that concerned us above all. As for the verdict—well, we are ready to accept it as it is, if the rest of the community is willing to abide by it.

While such a response seems surprisingly tepid, it probably represented a compromise between the fiery Boyarsky and the more restrained Zolotkoff. The editorial seems, finally, to have been an uneasy synthesis of outrage and ultimate faith in the legal system, a grimfaced knuckling under to the system with one final, insignificant note of outrage.

On the following day, the *Morning Journal*, more straightforwardly a socialist publication, was less restrained. Beneath the headline, "Protests Against Averbuch Verdict: Friends of the Jewish boy who was shot claim that the coroner was too biased—They demand further investigation," it wrote:

Neutral parties today criticized the verdict of the coroner's jury and, particularly, the manner in which the proceedings were conducted by Coroner Hoffman. It's claimed that Hoffman hadn't permitted testimony from the Averbuch side and that Shippy himself sat at Hoffman's side throughout the hearing, giving him instructions. Lawyer Ickes, who came to defend the dead man, declared that the coroner hadn't permitted him to examine the police witnesses and he had therefore wished to resign.

Ickes accomplished one thing, nonetheless. He completely shattered the police allegation that Averbuch had purchased a knife two days before the shooting. The police brought a pawnbroker, John Corbly, who testified that Averbuch bought these items from him on February 24th at 4:30 P.M. Eiler, cashier at the commission house where Averbuch worked, swore that at the time alleged by Corbly, Averbuch was still working at his job. [Eiler paid him his wages *after* 4:30 P.M.]

Despite the imbalance of 25 witnesses to one, the police did not prove their case. To the contrary. It was shown that Averbuch was no anarchist. Shippy could say only that he looked suspicious. [That's why he got scared.] As to why he couldn't overcome Averbuch, Shippy says that he was extraordinarily strong.

To the coroner, Shippy said that his son Harry had been shot as he wrestled with Averbuch. Earlier, he had said that Harry had been shot as he entered the room.

Jane Addams said she would not give up the fight. She said the coroner's verdict was worthless and that, in America, the dealings of the coroner are not respected.

There is no evidence, however, that Addams actively carried on the fight, particularly since Ickes, the man she hired, seemed to think the inquest had been a relative success.

The reason for the *Journal's* outrage is clear, however. It wanted the inquest to explore Averbuch's motive and personality. The inquest's sole purpose, however, was either to exonerate Shippy or to determine if a trial was needed to investigate Shippy's actions further. As such, the *Journal* and other publications could feel that the things they had most wanted to see answered were not even asked. In finding twenty-five witnesses who backed Shippy's version of the story and only one witness who denied it (presumably Olga Averbuch), the police may not have proved their case, but they did succeed in showing the jury that there wasn't enough cause to probe any of the unanswered questions. Where the *Courier* had seen the good in that—that the aspersions of anarchy, although not erased, would die through lack of further repetition—the *Journal* insisted on more: it wanted an apology. It would certainly never get it.

In the *Public* on March 28, Louis Post wrote a short piece on the subject out of a comparable sense of outrage:

> "We are ready to accept the verdict of the coroner's jury as it is, if the rest of the community is willing to abide by it." These are the measured words of the *Jewish Daily Courier*. They should sink deep into the minds of the whole people of Chicago. Is the rest of this community willing to abide by that verdict? In the interest of the due administration of justice let us hope not. If the proceedings before the coroner's jury are fairly reported, the investigation was a farce, having no other apparent object than the exoneration of the policeman who killed the boy; and unless the grand jury probes this case to the bottom, with neither the fear that seems to have paralyzed the Chicago bar nor the favor that seems to have influenced the coroner's investigation, human life may be regarded in Chicago as matter of small concern when it is a policeman who kills.

The source of Post's outrage was not that he, or his community, had been struck without apology or revenge; it was rather, as it was so often for him, that democracy was not functioning with the impartiality it would require to integrate all of Chicago into one great people. He saw in the inquest's having limited itself to the letter of its grand jury–like assignment a blow less to the law than to justice. And to him, any blow to justice was a victory for socialism or anarchy in that it demonstrated that the state as it was constructed could not guarantee the rights of all people equally.

From another vantage, anarchist Voltarine de Cleyre of Philadelphia insisted the Averbuch Affair was proof that American governance, in its root inequity, required periodic scapegoats. In the May issue of Emma Goldman's *Mother Earth* magazine, she wrote:

> It was a foregone conclusion that when a shivering, starving, half-crazed man killed a priest in Denver recently, he would be called an Anarchist. When a cowardly Chief of Police in Chicago, frightened no doubt by the memory of his blows upon the heads of unarmed workingmen walking in peaceful demonstrations, grappled in a spasm of terror, and killed a slender youth whose purpose in calling upon him is not known, and never will be known now, it was to be certainly anticipated that the boy would be denounced as an Anarchist, and the cold-blooded murder of him justified by that one word. And Shippy is exonerated by laying that word across his victim's body, though by his own law he should have been tried for murder![77]

De Cleyre insisted that Alia and Averbuch (and presumably Silverstein) were of a piece, individuals crushed by the state simply because the state would have to crush individuals periodically.[78]

The statements of the *Journal, Post,* de Cleyre, and any other individuals or publications that denounced the inquest fell on deaf ears. Coroner Hoffman, having walked a tightrope between the pressures of his political mentor and the concerns of an agitated public, was certainly not about to reopen proceedings. Schuettler, who continued in his role of de facto chief of police, was not about to pursue an investigation that insinuated his boss as well as his office were not the impartial upholders of law they claimed to be. Mayor Busse, a savvy politician, knew better than to confront controversy when it was just as easy to ignore it. The newspapers, sensing perhaps a weariness throughout their relationship with the case, could find other ways to boost their sales. No one with the influence to do anything about the affair ever spoke out. The inquest, inadequate as it certainly was, served as the final official word on the Averbuch Affair.

Even as there were individuals criticizing the inquest process, there were individuals intent on seeing the investigation continue. So far as the papers and the public were concerned, the mystery was past. So far as the police and city officials were concerned, there was no mystery. The individuals who continued trying to resolve the affair were thus critics of the police. Some spoke or wrote out of the paranoia typical of conspiracy theorists, while others grounded their explanations in the indisputable facts of the case. Some demonstrated their motives as growing out of social or political frameworks; others responded as Jews who felt one of their own had been maligned. As a whole, the different attempts to explain what happened and why constitute perhaps the most solid legacy of the Averbuch Affair. Emerging over the years, the differing explanations generally reveal more about their authors than they do about the case itself.

Philip Bregstone, a junior reporter for the *Jewish Courier* and author in 1930 of *Chicago and Its Jews*, speculated that Shippy may have gone into a murderous frenzy that morning because he had been drunk the night before. He writes:

> What actually happened at Thirty-One Lincoln Court, on February 2nd [*sic*], 1908, that brought the unfortunate boy to that home has remained a secret for these

past twenty-two years. It is not likely that the whole truth will ever be revealed. But some of the facts did come to light through the efforts of Peter Boyarsky and the *Courier* after George Shippy died a raving maniac in a sanitarium. A rumor became persistent that on the night previous to the Auerbach [*sic*] tragedy the Chief attended a banquet and did not return until the early hours of the morning. The eighteenth amendment was only a fancy then in the mind of some pious members of the Y.M.C.A. or the W.C.T.U. Perhaps if the amendment had been in existence, or if banquets had been occasions for speech making and eating only, Harry J. Auerbach's [*sic*] escape from the city of pogroms might not have been in vain.[79]

Such a theory is, of course, unlikely. Bregstone, like so many of his fellow temperance campaigners, demonized liquor far beyond its true character in order (unconsciously, probably) for it to serve as the primary excuse for the failings of American democracy. Even if Shippy had been drunk the evening before, it would not explain any erratic behavior the following morning—none, that is, beyond irritability or illness.

And yet, Bregstone does touch on a potentially critical issue with his theory: Shippy was clearly a man of enormous appetites. He was a big man, whose sympathetic biographers portrayed him as especially friendly with the men working beneath him in the fire and police departments. He was legendarily strong; one story has it that he used his shoulder to break through the door of Hyde Park's city hall when city workers in the former neighboring village locked it in fear they would lose their jobs once they had to answer to Chicago's city government. And he seems to have had a strong temper, hardly an unusual characteristic for a successful police officer.

What's more, Bregstone was correct that Shippy eventually died in a sanitarium. Shippy's dissolution did not come about through alcoholism, however. He was, rather, syphilitic. And, in the days before penicillin treatment, that was a fatal and horrible disease. In its advanced stages it did produce insanity and might well be the explanation for some sudden, violent impulse that led him to shoot, without investigating, a foreign-looking young man who had come knocking at his door. His disease also suggests that Shippy was not the upright family man Mayor Busse and other city officials would have wanted him to appear. He almost certainly contracted the disease in one of the many whorehouses that had proliferated throughout the city but were concentrated in the notorious First Ward. He may have been no more a part of the city's underworld than many a seemingly respectable man who went looking for thrills in Hinky-Dink's kingdom, but few of those other men were charged with shutting the kingdom down.

It is possible, then, that Shippy's rage that morning grew out of his incipient madness. It may well be that he suffered some form of hallucination or entered some berserk state that caused him to shoot Averbuch when the boy came unexpectedly to the door. That would explain Averbuch's killing, of course, but not the wounding of Harry Shippy, Foley, or Chief Shippy himself.

We are left, then, with very little to believe of the claims that some diabolical plot called for Averbuch to be killed as a means to a coverup. What legitimate questions there are in the shooting of Harry Shippy—Harry Shippy initially claimed he was shot coming down the stairs, but subsequent testimony and medical evidence revealed he had been shot from behind—aren't sufficient to doubt that Foley was shot randomly during a scuffle of some kind. That Chief Shippy's wounds were not nearly as serious as he first claimed is no basis to believe that they were self-inflicted. Whatever took place that morning took place with Averbuch at the center of it.

The question then concerns what happened when Shippy came to the door to meet Averbuch? Shippy claimed, of course, that he took the strange young man for an anarchist immediately. In one statement in the evening of the day Averbuch was shot he said, "I am confident this anarchist was an assassin who had been chosen by a band of his comrades to kill me because I have been making war on anarchists in Chicago." That suggested a tautology, of course: Averbuch was an anarchist because he had attempted to assassinate the chief, and we know he was bent on assassination because he was clearly an anarchist.

It is possible that Shippy actually thought something else and dared not report it to the public. He was, after all, somehow involved in the war then gripping the city between James O'Leary's and Mont Tennes's gangs. There is, in fact, evidence that he had thrown his support behind Tennes's gang. He could, then, have suspected his attacker was an assassin sent by O'Leary.

Shippy might also have taken Averbuch for one of the Black Hand terrorists then prevalent in the city. On the very day of the shooting, according to the *Inter Ocean*, Schuettler had been contacted concerning a Black Hand threat against a Waukegan laborer. He had apparently earned the enmity of the Black Hand for his efforts to break their cabal and had reported concerns that they might be preparing to kill him.

The trouble with either speculation—that Shippy might have taken Averbuch for a gangster or a Black Hand member rather than an anarchist—is that neither suggests any alternative to what took place inside Shippy's house that morning. Even if Shippy chose to paint his visitor in the most terrifying colors (and in a way that would do the least to implicate him in any illegal activities), his story holds essentially as he told it. He understood Averbuch to be an attacker and, in grappling with the boy, he killed him.

For all of the inconsistencies in Shippy's account of the struggle, then, we're left with the inescapable conclusion that the fight itself happened roughly as he described it. Whatever the particulars of who was hurt when, or what exactly he thought when he saw Averbuch at the door, the broad outline of the scuffle seems clear. Foley confirmed the story even with the serious wound he bore and, in a month of scrutiny, none of Shippy's family members ever suggested any version of the story that differs in any significant way from the original.

The crux of the mystery returns then, as it always must, to what Lazarus Averbuch's intentions were that morning. Many of Averbuch's supporters insist he entered the house unarmed, with no intention of hurting the chief. They claim that he was drawn there either out of some civil mission or by some mistaken understanding of the role of a United States police chief. Everything we know of Averbuch—admittedly quite little—suggests they are right.

The most popular theory for why Averbuch went to the chief's in the first place is that he needed a certificate of good conduct to find work elsewhere. But to accept that notion begs another question: Where did Averbuch expect to find other work opportunities? The likeliest answer seems to be that he had somehow made contact with Abraham Levy, who had made it his project to settle immigrant young men as farmers in the Midwest, particularly in Iowa. Levy's work was well known, the theory went, and Averbuch could quite easily have heard of it from his fellow Eichengreen employees or from talk on the street. He seemed the sort who would have been attracted to the opportunity; by all accounts a hard worker and a driven young man, he would likely have seen farming as a chance to work unfettered in a place where his labors would have been more readily recognized and rewarded.

Some others claimed that Averbuch might have hoped to travel even further west, to California. He might have heard general reports of job opportunities out there, or he might have mistaken the "Go West, young man" campaign—undertaken by such newspaper men as Horace Greeley and John L. B. Soule, among others—and the gold rush fever of sixty years before for news of the day. Someone as frustrated by his failure to find satisfying work as Averbuch was would likely have been attracted by the legend of a West Coast that gave birth to self-made men and dramatic fortunes.

While there is evidence to support both possibilities—although not a great deal—they too raise questions that stretch credibility. To begin with, it is difficult to imagine that Averbuch could have known of distant job opportunities without knowing at least the rudiments of American employment practices. It seems hard to believe that whoever told him there were farming opportunities in Iowa did not then answer what would most likely have been Averbuch's first question: "How do I go about getting there?" If he learned that jobs awaited him in California, he would almost certainly have learned that he needed to do nothing more than go to California and present himself as an able-bodied worker.

Even if his initial sources of information had neglected to tell him that most basic element of finding work, it is simply going too far to imagine that no one else would have told him. One of his friends at Eichengreen's and the foreman at the neighboring worksite both testified during the inquest that Averbuch had asked them how to get to Shippy's home. He would likely as well have discussed any plans he had with friends to know more about the American system than he did. Averbuch may have been green, but he would not have gone ignorant of his privileges as long as his supporters claim he did.

Even granting such a possibility is troubling, however, because it means that Olga Averbuch knew nothing, or quite little, of her brother's plans. Such ignorance on Olga's part, while terribly unlikely as well, would suggest that she and her brother were not as close as she led newspapers and supporters to believe. It shouldn't be surprising that the siblings might have drifted apart—Olga had been in the United States for three years and had not seen her brother since early adolescence before he joined her only three months before his death—but it does begin to undermine the bulwark of Averbuch's supporters' claims of his innocence.

Throughout the public obsession with the case and during the inquest itself, Olga was the only unambiguously favorable witness Averbuch had. She was the source of the reports that he was a "good boy" who would never have concerned himself with politics. She was the one who claimed her brother was an innocent victim of forces he knew nothing about. And she was the one whose wail of grief caught the ear of Jane Addams and other social activists and transformed his killing from a strictly political event into a tragedy with a human face. To propose that Averbuch seriously contemplated any travel plans of which he had told her almost nothing—plans advanced enough for him to have gone to Shippy's home in pursuit of them—is to question the only solid basis we have for believing in Averbuch's being so unlikely an assassin. Without Olga's claims, Averbuch looks no different to the world than Silverstein of New York or Alia of Denver.

It seems, then, that Averbuch may have gone to Shippy's home knowing what he was doing and who he was to visit. We can't know whether he was armed, although we can say with some certainty that he did not purchase any weapons from a pawnbroker. We know that he obtained the address from people at work and that he hopped a five-cent trolley car up Halsted Avenue to Chicago's near north side. We know that he rang the chief's door without any particular aggression and that he spoke at first to Shippy's daughter without betraying any evil purpose to her. We know also that minutes later he was dead.

Although we can't know what he was thinking that morning, it is virtually impossible to read through the material of the case and not come to some conclusion. So it is that we imagine Averbuch as he shuffled his feet on the chief's doormat, his heart racing as he prepared to knock at the imposing door before him. He is there not out of any developed political or social platform, but out of a primitive, childish urge to see something of the promise America had held out to him from Europe. He does not like the chief, but then he knows little of him. This is a mission of stubborn dignity, an insistence that he be regarded as a human being and an attempt to confirm that his dreams count for something.

He has things to ask the chief. Why cannot unemployed men be free to march in protest of their circumstances? Why cannot Emma Goldman be permitted the free speech so clearly promised by the country's basic documents? He may even ask the chief for help in finding a job with responsibility and good pay. Surely the chief would be of help to an honest and hard-working young man like himself.

He is not certain how the chief will receive him. He hopes the chief will be civil. He has been treated roughly by officials before, though, and he knows he won't suffer much for being thrown back out through the door.

He straightens the good jacket he is wearing and pats his pockets. He feels the paper on which he has written 31 Lincoln Place.

He feels also the silly exercises he has practiced at school, practiced enough to know that they are not the avenue to the ambitions he nurses. He feels perhaps a gun, perhaps not. In any case, he has no intention of using it. He's not here to hurt anyone. He is here, finally, because he needs to know some horizon beyond the squalid ghetto in which he finds himself trapped. He is like the child pressing his face up to the candy store glass, grown bold enough at last to reach defiantly for one perfectly iced éclair. He has left the Chicago of the near West Side and its immigrant poverty for the Chicago of wealth, power, and prestige; the Chicago promised to him in the days when he and his family dodged torch-wielding Cossacks and fled from the pogroms that killed so many of the people he knew. He has given only partial thought to what he must ask the chief, and he has told no one that he has gone. He knows for certain only that he is reaching out for the life that has continually eluded him, that the man who lives here is a symbol both of the wealth he cannot begin to work toward and of the police power that so persistently succeeds in keeping him down.

And so it is that he stands in his best clothes on a Monday morning before Chief Shippy's door. From a distance he must look like any other caller, any acquaintance of the chief's come to drop by for a quick chat. It would take a passerby some staring to recognize that he is not of this neighborhood, that he is in a Chicago very different from the one he knows. He looks—and perhaps very quickly feels—like a real American.

And so he knocks at the door.

AFTERWORD

The Averbuch Affair is fascinating in part because it touched on so many lives from so many different worlds. The best-known characters figuring in the events went on to well-documented careers, while many of those least known faded almost without a trace into history. Some of the affair's central figures were left little touched by what happened, while others would never be the same again.

The Shippy family was left in shambles. Chief Shippy would recover from his injuries quickly—as quickly as if he had never received them—but he would never again be the feared chief of police. Without ever entirely reassuming his duties, he resigned as chief a couple of months after the affair. Within a year and a half he voluntarily admitted himself to a sanitarium, and within several years he died while acting, according to press reports, like a "raving maniac."[80]

Harry Shippy, too, would recover from his injuries eventually, but it would take him considerably longer than his father.

He returned to school within the year and continued to make progress toward graduation. In 1915, he died suddenly from a burst appendix.[81]

Mrs. Shippy saw to it that her husband and son were buried side by side—their graves are impressive still in Oakwoods Cemetery—but she then appears to have left Chicago and she never returned for any length of time. Neither she nor her daughter is buried next to her husband and son.

Herman Schuettler had a happier path. Although he was not appointed to succeed Shippy as chief—an irony considering he had been the effective chief for months—he did eventually succeed to the position. Although he is not often recalled today, he left behind a reputation as a tough but competent police officer. He may well have represented some of what was worst in turn-of-the-century administrators in his unexamined elitism and racism, but he also was a man who defended the only Chicago he knew with intelligence and integrity.

Averbuch's various supporters went a number of different paths. Jane Addams, of course, lived on to continue speaking out for compassion and understanding. Her Nobel Peace Prize in 1931 capped the career of one of the great humanitarians Chicago or any city has ever known.

Harold Ickes continued his career as a Chicago newsman, a key figure in the Progressive Party, and a fierce independent in Chicago politics. He rose to national and international fame as President Franklin Roosevelt's secretary of the interior. In this position he became an outspoken early critic of the Nazi regime in Germany and was loathed and detested by them. His greatest claim to fame, however, came in his opinionated defense of America's national resources and parks. His tenure lasted through the entire New Deal years, and he finally resigned amid great controversy after Harry Truman was elected President. Ickes died in 1952.

Emma Goldman and Ben Reitman continued touring the country together for years. Their tempestuous relationship ended about a decade after the Averbuch Affair had brought them together. Reitman returned to Chicago and settled into a career as one of the city's best-known characters. Legend has it he served as whorehouse physician to the Capone gang and that he made himself a favorite of the odd collection of free thinkers, socialists, and sociopaths who frequented the Dill Pickle Club and Bug House Square near the Newberry Library. Goldman remained a firebrand until the day she died. After the end of World War I, U.S. officials managed at last to force her out of the country, and she sought refuge in the Soviet Union. An early advocate of the Bolshevik revolution, she soon proved too much of a critic there as well and was deported by the Soviets in 1923.

Boyarsky and Zolotkoff, the *Courier* reporters, had their separate difficulties. Boyarsky died suddenly not long after the Averbuch Affair; he had insisted that he be given no tribute and that he be buried in the potter's field among the poor and downtrodden with whom he had always sympathized. Zolotkoff's ambition took him to New York and Palestine, where he never achieved the same distinction he won so early in Chicago. He tried his hand as a fiction writer, but his work is long forgotten.

Olga Averbuch never recovered from her grief at losing her brother. Crushed at what she had seen, she decided to return to Europe and to what was left of her family. What happened to her thereafter is impossible to determine, but it seems likely she suffered the fate of most Jews who found themselves in Hitler's Europe. Although there is no record of her fate, many of the Jews of Czernowitz died at Auschwitz. Before she vanished altogether, though, she wrote a final letter to Ickes, thanking him and telling of her grief. That letter serves as a coda to the entire Averbuch Affair:

Czernowitz, 9/23, 1908

Highly Honored Sir,

The arrival at home was as terrible for me as the
sight of my dead brother. My poor mother still hoped
to see her son once more and the moment when she
saw me alone was dreadful. The crushed poor old
woman cannot understand why they killed her dear
son. She sent him to America with heavy heart, but she
had the hope that by his labor he would become the
support of his old parents. My poor mother begs that
good and noble men take up the cause of her innocent
son. She says that they have taken everything from her
with this child, that these few years which she should
have passed in peace have been disturbed by the death
of her son. "It is impossible to understand how such a
thing can happen in free America and go unavenged.
My poor child is dead and feels nothing, but my life
and that of my husband and children is wrecked. Day
and night we bewail the death of our loved child, which
was our hope. This bitter pain is nigh unendurable.
The murderer who goes about in freedom not only
killed my son; he poisoned the lives of a family of eight
persons. There must be some justice in America and it
would be a slight comfort to me if the court should
declare that my son died innocent.
    "I am eternally grateful to the good and noble
ladies and gentlemen who came to the help of my poor
daughter in this great misfortune. May God reward
them for the many services they rendered my daughter
and for giving her the means to come here where I can
see her. Thousand, thousand thanks."
    I have to tell you, my dear Sir, that the voyage did
me good and quieted my nerves. Now I am compelled
to work hard in order to help my parents who live very
poorly. My two sisters work too, because my brothers

are too young to work and earn anything, and my parents who are old and weak, have been utterly crushed by this blow. Should you, highly honored Sir, perhaps desire further information about that matter, I shall supply you with addresses of respected men with whom he formerly was and indeed about his whole previous life. I shall be grateful to you as long as I live if you will take the trouble of establishing the innocence of my dear unfortunate brother. I had always hoped that I should find a support in him, but now I must begin work anew. I do not know whether I can keep it up; my nerves are completely shattered by these recent events, particularly by my imprisonment (arrest).

I beg you, honored Sir, not to forget me or my poor unfortunate brother. Please express my most heartfelt thanks, as also those of my whole family, to Miss Addams and Miss Field.

Eternally your thankful,
Olga

Should you be good enough to write me, I ask that it be in German, if possible.[82]

The most poignant element of Olga's letter is her plea that her brother's death not be forgotten. Her appeal to Ickes to continue his efforts to clear Lazarus's name seems to have grown as much out of her fear that the entire affair would be forgotten as it did out of any sustained hope that she might still see justice. She seemed to sense that the fickle attentions of the American public had shifted elsewhere. Ickes himself may have claimed that he had succeeded in keeping Coroner Hoffman from officially labeling Averbuch an anarchist, but he had clearly failed to change the public perception. Whatever the facts may have shown—and they do not show that Averbuch had any connection to anar-chists—they could not persuade the bulk of Chicago to think Averbuch was anything other than a political assassin. In this fi-nal letter, Olga Averbuch seems to have sensed that her brother's death would one day be almost entirely forgotten, and she pleaded that it not be.

We hope this book in some way answers her plea.

ENDNOTES

Preface

1. Throughout the course of the Averbuch affair, there was controversy about the correct English form of Averbuch's first name. Although the best source on the subject—Averbuch's sister Olga—insisted his name should be either Jeremiah or Harry, we have opted in this book to use Lazarus since it was the form most widely used by the media of the day.

2. A. James Rudin, "From Kishinev to Chicago: The Forgotten Story of Lazar Averbuch," *Midstream* vol. 18, no. 7 (August/September 1972).

Chapter I

3. For information on the Miriam Club, see H. L. Meites, *History of the Jews of Chicago* (Chicago: Chicago Jewish Historical Society Press, 1990), 208–9, 629.

4. Meites, 160–62.

5. Meites, 159–60, 168.

6. For information on Shippy's life, see the *Chicago Tribune*, April 14, 1907; A.T. Andreas, *History of Chicago*, vol. 3 (Chicago: A. T. Andreas Co., 1886), 122; and Newton Bateman and Paul Selby, *Historical Encyclopedia of Illinois, Cook County Edition*, vol. 2, (Chicago: Munsell Publishing Co., 1905), 996–97.

7. Harry Barnard, *The Forging of an American Jew: The Life and Times of Judge Julian W. Mack* (New York: Herzl Press, 1974), 85-88.

8. Robert J. Goldstein, "The Anarchist Scare of 1908: A Sign of Tensions in the Progressive Era" *American Studies* 15 (Fall 1974), 55-78. See also Paul Avrich, *Anarchists Portraits* (Princeton, N.J.: Princeton University Press, 1988).

9. Roger A. Bruns, *The Damndest Radical: The Life and World of Ben Reitman, Chicago's Celebrated Social Reformer, Hobo King and Whorehouse Physician* (Urbana: University of Illinois Press, 1987), 51–57.

10. Bruns, 55–56.

11. For a complete history of the Tennes-O'Leary showdown, see John Landesco, *Organized Crime in Chicago*, originally published in 1929 as Part III of the *Illinois Crime Survey* (Chicago: University of Chicago Press, 1968), 45–83. For more detailed information on Kenna's connection to organized gambling interests, see Lloyd Wendt and Herman Kogan, *Lords of the Levee: The Story of Bathhouse John and Hinky Dink* (Garden City, N.Y.: Garden City Publishing Co., 1944).

12. Landesco, 46.

13. Landesco, 49.

Chapter II

14. *Chicago Daily Journal,* March 2, 1908.

15. For a full examination of Altgeld's role in the Haymarket affair, see Harry Barnard, *The Eagle Forgotten: The Life of John Peter Altgeld* (Secaucus, N.J.: Lyle Stuart, 1938).

16. Jane Addams, "The Chicago Settlements and Social Unrest." *Charities and Commons* 20 (May 2, 1908); 155–66.

Chapter III

17. Ed Baumann and John O'Brien, "The Sausage Factory Mystery," *Chicago Tribune*, August 3, 1986.

18. *Chicago Inter Ocean*, March 3, 1908.

19. *Chicago Tribune*, March 3, 1908.

20. *Chicago Daily News*, March 3, 1908.

21. *Chicago Inter Ocean*, March 3, March 7, and March 13, 1908.

22. *Chicago Daily News*, March 2, 1908.

Chapter IV

23. Goldstein, 63–84.

24. For more information on Louis Post, see his obituaries, *New York Times* and *Chicago Tribune* (January 11, 1921), and an appreciation in *The Nation* 126 (January 25, 1928), 83.

25. Barbara Newell, *Chicago and the Labor Movement* (Urbana: University of Illinois Press, 1961), 17–26.

26. For an analysis of Addams's liberal philosophy within the context of the Averbuch affair, see Daniel Levine, *Jane Addams and the Liberal Tradition* (Madison: State Historical Society of Wisconsin, 1971), 148–52. For a firsthand recollection of the particular pressures that Hull House faced in the wake of the affair, see Alice Hamilton, *Exploring the Dangerous Trades: Labor Reform in the Progressive Era: The Autobiography of Alice Hamilton, M.D.* (Boston: Little, Brown and Co., 1943), 78–79.

27. For more information on Taylor, see Louise Wade, *Graham Taylor: Pioneer for Social Justice 1851–1938* (Chicago: University of Chicago Press, 1964). For more information on Mary McDowell, see Howard Wilson, *Mary McDowell, Neighbor* (Chicago: University of Chicago Press, 1928).

28. Bruns, 38–39.

29. Emma Goldman, *Living My Life* (Salt Lake City: A Peregrine Smith Book/ Gibbs M. Smith, Inc., 1982), 414.

30. Goldman, 6–10.

Chapter V

31. Edgar Bernhard, Ira Latimer, and Harvey O'Connor discuss the Averbuch affair in the context of broad anti-Semitism in Chicago in 1907–1908 in *Pursuit of Freedom: A History of Civil Liberty in Illinois, 1787–1942* (Chicago: Chicago Civil Liberties Committee/ Illinois Civil Liberties Committee, 1942), 121.

32. Isaac Levitals, "The Story of the Chicago Jewish Community" (Chicago: Chicago Board of Jewish Education, 1954, mimeograph), 12.

33. The fullest record of Chicago's early German Jews is in Meites and in Irving Cutler, *The Jews of Chicago: From Shtetl to Suburb* (Urbana: University of Illinois Press, 1996). Also useful is Philip Bregstone, *Chicago and Its Jews* (Chicago: n.p., 1933).

34. For overviews of the East European Jewish presence in Chicago, see Edward Mazur, "Jewish Chicago: From Diversity to Community," in *Ethnic Chicago*, revised and expanded edition, ed. Melvin Holli and Peter d'A. Jones (Grand Rapids, Mich.: William B. Eerdmans Publishing Co., 1984); and Irving Cutler, *The Jews of Chicago: From Shtetl to Suburb* (Urbana: University of Illinois Press, 1996). For a detailed discussion of the Maxwell Street Market, see Ira Berkow, *Maxwell Street: Survival in a Bazaar* (Garden City, N.J.: Doubleday, 1977).

35. Newspaper reports throughout the Averbuch Affair report instances of anonymous donations made in sympathy with Averbuch. Harry Barnard underscores that point in his biography of Julian Mack, *The Forging of an American Jew*, 87, when he describes the tension some mainstream Jews felt when confronted with the opportunity to attend Averbuch's funeral. See also Seymour Pomrenze, "Aspects of Chicago Russian-Jewish Life, 1893–1915," *The Chicago Pinkas*, ed. Simon Rawidowicz (Chicago: College of Jewish Studies, 1952), 117, for a further description of the way German Jews distributed charity to the newer Russian and Eastern European arrivals. See also the *Chicago Inter Ocean*, March 11, 1908.

36. Bregstone, 184.

37. Bregstone, 181.

38. Bernard Horwich, *My First Eighty Years* (Chicago: Argus Books, 1939), 262–65.

Chapter VI

39. *New York Morning Journal,* March 12. 1908.

Chapter VII

40. Unpublished personal memoir from the papers of Harold Ickes, Library of Congress, 6.

41. Harold Ickes, *The Autobiography of a Curmudgeon* (New York: Reynal and Hitchcock, 1943), 115.

42. Goldman, 416.

43. Ickes memoir, 6–11.

44. For the fullest published treatment of the Averbuch inquest, see T. H. Watkins, *Righteous Pilgrim: The Life and Times of Harold L. Ickes* (New York: Henry Holt and Co., 1990), 93–99.

45. Horwich, 264–65.

Chapter VIII

46. For further details about the role of Jewish gangsters and boxers in defending Chicago Jews against ethnic attacks, see Walter Roth, "The Story of Samuel 'Nails' Morton: A 20th Century Chicago Golem?" *Chicago Jewish History* 13 (October 1989). See also Robert Rockaway, *But—He Was Good to His Mother: The Lives and Crimes of Jewish Gangsters,* especially chapter 8, "Defenders of Their People" (Jerusalem: Gefen Publishing House, 1993).

47. Jane Addams, "The Chicago Settlements and Social Unrest," *Charities and Commons,* vol. 20, April–October 1908, 157.

48. Barnard, *The Forging of An American Jew*, 87.

49. Meites refers frequently to Hirsch throughout his *History of the Jews of Chicago*. See pp. 155–56 in particular for the boast that Hirsch was "the highest-salaried rabbi in the world."

50. This is, of course, merely an educated guess. Rosenwald frequently played an ambassadorial role in articulating the concerns of Chicago's Jews before the mainstream American media. For more information, see M. R. Werner, *Julius Rosenwald: The Life of a Practical Humanitarian* (New York: Harper and Brothers, 1939).

Chapter IX

51. William Preston, *Aliens and Dissenters: Federal Suppression of Radicals, 1903–1933* (Cambridge: Harvard University Press, 1963), 11–34.

52. For a good overview of the legislative and social battles over immigration, see John Higham, *Send These to Me: Immigrants in Urban America*, rev. ed. (Baltimore: Johns Hopkins University Press, 1984). See especially chapter 2, "The Politics of Immigration Restriction."

53. *Congressional Record*, vol. 42, 60th Congress, March 2, 1908, 2755.

54. Bregstone, 183.

55. *Congressisonal Record*, 2933.

56. *Congressional Record*, 3494.

57. *Congressional Record*, 3592.

58. *Congressional Record*, 3652.

59. *New York Times*, March 4, 1908.

60. Oscar Straus, *Under Four Administrations: From Cleveland to Taft* (Boston: Houghton Mifflin Co., 1922), 233–34.

61. *Congressional Record*, 2757.

62. Walter Roth, "Forced Return of Russian Jewish Immigrant Prevented—1908," *Society News of the Chicago Jewish Historical Society* 12 (December 1988).

63. *Morning Journal*, March 10.

64. Richard Drinnon, *Rebel in Paradise* (Chicago: University of Chicago Press, 1961), 124.

65. Goldman, 421. For a detailed description of Goldman's affair with Reitman, see *In Love, Anarchy and Emma Goldman* (New York: Holt, Rinehart and Winston, 1984).

66. *Chicago Inter Ocean*, March 17, 1908.

67. Goldman, 422–23.

Chapter X

68. Ickes memoir, 10.

69. The records and files of the inquest proceedings and police investigations are not available from the coroner's office. They were either lost or have disappeared. A diligent search, including a request under the Freedom of Information Act, indicates that all official transcripts and files relating to the case are not available. Accounts that are cited from the inquest were taken from either the March 25, 1908 issue of the the *Chicago Daily News* or the *Chicago Inter Ocean*.

70. *ChicagoTribune*, March 25, 1908.

71. Ickes memoir, 12.

72. Ickes memoir, 12–15.

73. Ickes memoir, 10–11.

74. Ickes memoir, 7.

75. The death certificate issued by the Cook County coroner's office notes that Averbuch died from "gunshot wounds, said wounds inflicted by bullets fired from revolvers held in the hands of Geo. Shippy and Jas. Foley." The certificate was not issued until April 17, and it makes no mention of anarchy. It bears the signature of Coroner Peter Hoffman.

Chapter XI

76. For an early instance linking Averbuch with Alia, see "Anarchy at Work," *The World Today: A Monthly Record of Human Progress,* vol. 14, (December 1907-June 1908): Chicago: 348–49. For one linking Averbuch and Silverstein, see "Editorial," *American Hebrew and Jewish Messenger,* (April 3, 1908). For a critical look at the tendency to collapse the three anarchist events, see Goldstein, "The Anarchist Scare of 1908: A Sign of Tensions in the Progressive Era," *American Studies* 15, (1974): 58–78.

77. Voltairine de Cleyre, "Open Your Eyes," *Mother Earth* 3, (May 1908): 156–59.

78. For more on de Cleyre, see Paul Avrich, *An American Anarchist: The Life of Voltairine de Cleyre* (Princeton, N.J.: Princeton University Press, 1978).

79. Bregstone, 186.

Afterword

80. See the obituary headlined, "Shippy Funeral Held Tomorrow: Former Chief Succumbs at His Residence from Softening of the Brain," *Chicago Tribune,* April 14, 1913.

81. *Chicago Evening American,* April 20, 1915.

82. Jane Addams Papers, Series 1, Supplement, Swarthmore College Peace Collection.

BIBLIOGRAPHY

Addams, Jane. "The Chicago Settlements and Social Unrest." *Charities and Commons* 20 (April–October 1908): 155–66.

———. Papers. Series 1, Supplement. Swarthmore College Peace Collection.

American Hebrew and Jewish Messenger (April 3, 1908).

Andreas, A. T. *History of Chicago.* Vol. 3. Chicago: A. T. Andreas Co., 1886.

Avrich, Paul. *An American Anarchist: The Life of Voltairine de Cleyre.* Princeton, N.J.: Princeton University Press, 1978.

———. *Anarchists Portraits.* Princeton, N.J.: Princeton University Press, 1988.

Barnard, Harry. *The Eagle Forgotten: The Life of John Peter Atgeld.* 1966. Reprint. Secaucus, N.J.: Lyle Stuart, 1973.

———. *The Eagle Forgotten: The Life of John Peter Atgeld.* Rev. ed. Secaucus, N.J.: Lyle Stuart, 1973.

———. *The Forging of an American Jew: The Life and Times of Judge Julian W. Mack.* New York: Herzl Press, 1974.

Bateman, Newton, and Paul Selby. *Historical Encyclopedia of Illinois, Cook County Edition.* Vol. 2. Chicago: Munsell Publishing Co., 1905.

Berkow, Ira. *Maxwell Street: Survival in a Bazaar.* Garden City, N.J.: Doubleday, 1977.

Bernhard, Edgar, Ira Latimer, and Harvey O'Connor. *Pursuit of Freedom: A History of Civil Liberty in Illinois, 1787–1942.* Chicago: Chicago Civil Liberties Committee/Illinois Civil Liberties Committee, 1942.

Bregstone, Philip. *Chicago and Its Jews.* Chicago: n.p., 1933.

Bruns, Roger A. *The Damndest Radical: The Life and World of Ben Reitman, Chicago's Celebrated Social Reformer, Hobo King and Whorehouse Physician.* Urbana: University of Illinois Press, 1987.

Chicago Daily News, March 2, 1908.

———, March 3, 1908.

Chicago Evening American, April 20, 1915.

Chicago Inter Ocean, March 3, 1908.

———, March 7, 1908.

———, March 11, 1908.

———, March 13, 1908.

———, March 17, 1908.

———, March 25, 1908.

Chicago Tribune, April 14, 1907.

———, March 3, 1908.

———, March 25, 1908.

———, April 14, 1913.

———, August 3, 1986.

Congressional Record. 60th Cong., March 2, 1908. Vol. 42.

Cutler, Irving. *The Jews of Chicago: From Shtetl to Suburb.* Urbana: University of Illinois Press, 1996.

Daily Journal. March 2, 1908.

de Cleyre, Voltairine. "Open Your Eyes." *Mother Earth* 3 (May 1908).

Drinnon, Richard. *Rebel in Paradise.* Chicago: University of Chicago Press, 1961.

Falk, Candace. "Love Like a Mighty Spectre." *In Love, Anarchy and Emma Goldman.* New York: Holt, Rinehart and Winston, 1984.

Goldman, Emma. *Living My Life.* Salt Lake City: A Peregrine Smith Book/Gibbs M. Smith, Inc. 1982.

Goldstein, Robert. "The Anarchist Scare of 1908: A Sign of Tensions in the Progressive Era." *American Studies* 15: 1974, 55–78.

————. *Political Repression in America.* Cambridge, Mass.: Schenkman Publishing Co., 1978.

Hamilton, Alice. *Exploring the Dangerous Trades: Labor Reform in the Progressive Era: The Autobiography of Alice Hamilton, M. D.* Boston: Little, Brown and Co., 1943.

Higham, John. *Send These to Me: Immigrants in Urban America.* Rev. ed. Baltimore: Johns Hopkins University Press, 1984.

Horwich, Bernard. *My First Eighty Years.* Chicago: Argus Books, 1939.

Ickes, Harold. *The Autobiography of a Curmudgeon.* New York: Reynal and Hitchcock, 1943.

————. Unpublished Personal Memoirs. Library of Congress.

Landesco, John. *Organized Crime in Chicago.* Originally published in 1929 as Part III of *Illinois Crime Survey.* Chicago: University of Chicago Press, 1968.

Levine, Daniel. *Jane Addams and the Liberal Tradition.* Madison: State Historical Society of Wisconsin, 1971.

Levitats, Isaac. "The Story of the Chicago Jewish Community." Chicago: Chicago Board of Jewish Education, 1954. Mimeograph.

Mazur, Edward. "Jewish Chicago: From Diversity to Community." In *Ethnic Chicago.* Rev. ed. Edited by Melvin Holli and Peter d'A. Jones. Grand Rapids, Mich.: William B. Eerdmans Publishing Co., 1984.

Meites, H. L. *History of the Jews of Chicago.* 1923. Reprint, Chicago: Chicago Jewish Historical Society Press, 1990.

New York Morning Journal, March 10, 1908.

———— March 12, 1908.

New York Times, March 4, 1908.

Newell, Barbara. *Chicago and the Labor Movement.* Urbana: University of Illinois Press, 1961.

Pomrenze, Seymour. "Aspects of Chicago Russian-Jewish Life, 1893–1915." *The Chicago Pinkas.* Edited by Simon Rawidowicz. Chicago: College of Jewish Studies, 1952.

Preston, William. *Aliens and Dissenters: Federal Suppression of Radicals, 1903–1933.* Cambridge: Harvard University Press, 1963.

Record Herald, March 25, 1908.

Rockaway, Robert. *But—He Was Good to His Mother: The Lives and Crimes of Jewish Gangsters.* Jerusalem: Gefen Publishing House, 1993.

Roth, Walter. "Forced Return of Russian Jewish Immigrant Prevented—1908." *Chicago Jewish History* 11 (December 1988).

————. "The Story of Samuel 'Nails' Morton: A 20th Century Chicago Golem?" *Chicago Jewish History* 13, (October 1989).

Rudin, A. James. "From Kishinev to Chicago: The Forgotten Story of Lazar Averbuch." *Midstream* (August/September 1972).

Straus, Oscar. *Under Four Administrations: From Cleveland to Taft.* Boston: Houghton Mifflin Co., 1922.

The World Today: A Monthly Record of Human Progress 14 (December 1907–June 1908).

Wade, Louise. *Graham Taylor: Pioneer for Social Justice 1851–1938.* Chicago: University of Chicago Press, 1964.

Watkins, T. H. *Righteous Pilgrim: The Life and Times of Harold L. Ickes.* New York: Henry Holt and Co., 1990.

Wendt, Lloyd, and Herman Kogan. *Lords of the Levee: The Story of Bathhouse John and Hinky Dink.* Garden City, N.Y.: Garden City Publishing Co., 1944.

Werner, M. R. *Julius Rosenwald: The Life of a Practical Humanitarian.* New York: Harper and Brothers, 1939.

Wilson, Howard. *Mary McDowell, Neighbor.* Chicago: University of Chicago Press, 1928.

INDEX

Index of Newspapers and Magazines

ABOUT THE AUTHORS

Joe Kraus and Walter Roth

Walter Roth is a senior partner of the law firm of D'Ancona & Pflaum, a firm of approximately eighty attorneys practicing civil law in Chicago, Illinois. He graduated from the University of Chicago law school, *summa cum laude*. He was managing editor of the *University of Chicago Law Review*. He also attended the University of Illinois, where he majored in history and journalism. Mr. Roth has been an officer and director of many business and civic organizations. He is currently president of the Chicago Jewish Historical Society. He has written many articles on Chicago history and has been published in *Chicago Jewish History*, the *Sentinel*, and *JUF News*.

Joe Kraus is the editor of *Chicago Jewish History*, the journal of the Chicago Jewish Historical Society, and a Ph.D. candidate in American literature at Northwestern University. He has been an instructor at Northwestern University, Roosevelt University, Columbia College (Chicago), Spertus Institute of Jewish Studies, Harry S. Truman College of the Chicago City Colleges System, and the International Academy of Merchandising and Design. He has published articles in the *American Scholar*, the *Prohibition Era Times*, and *Chicago Jewish History*. Kraus received his MA in English literature from Columbia University (New York) and his AB from the University of Michigan.